P9-BYD-888

FORWARD

FORWARD

a memoir

ABBY WAMBACH

DEY ST.
An Imprint of WILLIAM MORROW

The names of some of the individuals featured throughout this book have been changed to protect their privacy.

HarperCollins books may be purchased for educational, business, or sales promotional use. For information, please email the Special Markets Department at SPsales@harpercollins.com.

FIRST EDITION

Library of Congress Cataloging-in-Publication Data has been applied for.

ISBN 978-0-06-246698-3 (hardcover)
ISBN 978-0-06-265134-1 (Barnes & Noble Signed Edition)
ISBN 978-0-06-265135-8 (Books-A-Million Signed Edition)

16 17 18 19 20 DIX/RRD 10 9 8 7 6 5 4 3 2 1

Dear Abby,

Before there was soccer, championships, applause, jeers, heartbreak, shame: there you were, 4 years old. Today I want to hold you and promise you this:

Don't try to earn your worthiness. It's your birth-right.
Fear not failure. There is no such thing.
You will know real love. The journey will be long,
but you'll find your way home.
You are so brave, little one. I'm proud of you.

Love, Abby

"There is no greater agony than bearing
an untold story inside you."
—Zora Neale Hurston, *Dust Tracks on the Road*

CONTENTS

CONTENTS

1

FRAUD

I have scored more professional soccer goals than anyone in the history of the game, 184 to be exact, but I never once witnessed the ball hit the net. Although my eyes were open and aimed in the right direction, as soon as leather met rope the picture went black—not a slow fade, but a swift guillotine chop that separated the scene from my ability to see it.

My mind celebrated while my vision, blinded from adrenaline, lagged a beat behind, and by the time the two equalized there was a party on the field: high fives and *hell yeahs*, upraised arms and pumping legs and bouncing ponytails. I thrived on these brief blackouts, these zaps of instant amnesia. For thirty years scoring goals was my currency, the one skill I could barter for security and acceptance and love.

Rarely did my frenetic brain pause long enough to consider what might come next, and how the shape of my life would look without soccer to fill it up.

Now it's November 2015, two weeks after I announced my retirement, and my life is in no shape at all. President Obama recently called me and my teammates "badass" and I feel entirely unworthy of the term. I either sleep for 12-hour stretches or not at all, roaming the hallways of my hotel or impulse shopping online. The only time I break a sweat is when I hustle to the minibar. I am at my heaviest weight, my hibernation weight. I am cultivating Olympic-caliber love handles. ABBY WAMBACH HAS A SERIOUS BAKED GOODS ADDICTION, reports espn.com, and it's a charge I can't deny. Room service delivers at least one basket of muffins per day. In an effort to carb-shame myself, I Instagram every one that touches my lips, accompanied by self-flagellating hashtags: #cantstop. #socialpressure. #onedayatatime.

It doesn't work. I remain unashamed. The muffins keep coming. I study old pictures of myself—American flag draped over sculpted arms, face tipped up to the cheering crowd—and marvel not only at my physique but at my expression; I look much happier than I was.

There's a good chance that last night's mixed drinks amounted to a half bottle of vodka, chased by red wine and garnished with some Ambien. Five months ago, at the World Cup final, my wife Sarah and I made international news with a celebration kiss, and now she isn't speaking to me. We'd renovated a beautiful, sprawling house tucked in the hills outside of Portland, Oregon, and I can't even consider it home. I'm thirty-five years old and had planned on being pregnant by now. My body feels like a foreign object and I am desperate to escape my own mind. My two prime dueling emotions are misery and terror. If my life were currently on the roster, I would force it to do suicide runs up and down the field. I would make my life ride the bench. I might even cut it from the team.

I argue with myself: *You've been here before. You've had your heart broken. You've been depressed. You've been afraid. You've faced change.* And the unspoken response comes: *This time is different. This time there's permanence. This time you don't have soccer waiting for you, and you'll never have soccer again.*

I have relinquished soccer, but it has not relinquished me. I am still an ambassador of the sport, called upon to extol its virtues and translate its language. Today I'm scheduled to speak at a fundraiser for children's programs. I am expected to be fun and upbeat and inspirational, qualities that, once upon a time, came naturally to me. When the driver picks me up I realize I don't even know where I am: it could be Milwaukee or Nashville or Houston. I stare out the window, watching the streetscape blur past, and think, These are kids; I don't want to lie.

I am a terrible liar.

The field house is dimly lit. A single spotlight aims its beam at my head as if to illuminate the mess within. This moment is the opposite of instant amnesia, that thrilling shot of adrenaline that temporarily blinds me; this is anti-adrenaline, and I can see the kids all too clearly—hundreds of sweet, earnest faces and compact bodies squirming in anticipation. They are lined up in neat rows, looking like shots I'm bound to miss. The host introduces me with words that seem to apply to someone else: two-time Olympic gold medalist; FIFA World Player of the Year; winner of the Women's World Cup; record breaker; leader; legend.

I don't memorize speeches or even write them out, much to my mother's perennial dismay, but I have a rough chronology at the ready, a tour through my childhood and club career and time on the national team, a quick dip into challenges and triumphs, a hint at my future. But the kids don't want to hear a detailed exposition of my résumé. They want to know how they can be just like me when they grow up.

"You need to make a plan," I tell them. "You need to create your life."

Beneath these words a commentary begins scrolling through my brain, silent subtitles that negate everything I say aloud.

You can't even do that for yourself.

"You have every opportunity to do what you want in life. The whole world is open to you if you are brave enough to explore it."

You are barely brave enough to leave your hotel room.

"You have to be confident in your ability to do the right things, make the right choices."

You are incapable of living your own words. It's only a matter of time before you're exposed as the phony you are.

"Believe in yourself and you can change the world!"

They love me. I fold myself in half to give them high fives. They want to know they'll still have access to me, that my absence from the field doesn't mean I'll disappear altogether. I assure them, this time with conviction, that I am not going anywhere.

Today, my life still isn't what I'd once imagined, but I'm starting to appreciate the view. Soon after that event, I went for a run—just me gunning it uphill, feet batting against the road, fingers slicing the air, checking the data on my watch to ensure maximum effort, a twenty-year habit I'll never break. I considered it a great personal triumph when I posted a photo of a pristine, intact muffin with the hashtag: #enough isenough. Out of necessity, I took an extended break from the vodka. My body became familiar again and I waded, tentatively, back into my mind. For the first time in years it felt still and calm, and it whispered something I had never heard it say: *I can make an impact off the field.*

I let myself start to believe it.

In these pages I will share plenty of tales from the field—ones I have never told before—but this is not, at its core, a book about soccer. Because no matter who you are or what you've done with your life, you recognize the feeling I've described, that private, flailing terror that makes you wonder if you're lost for good. You have, at some point, been flattened and immobile and forced to find a way to reanimate yourself.

You've found yourself in the midst of transition, working up the nerve to release one rung and swing to the next, hoping to find some magic in the middle. You have been treated unfairly and unequally. You have been labeled, placed into ill-fitting boxes and told by others what you are and how to be. You have even labeled yourself, blunting your potential with your own words.

Here are just a few of my labels: tomboy, dyke, lesbian, butch, bitch, coward, failure, control freak, rebel, fraud. And a few more, on the flip side: phenom, inspiration, captain, champion, advocate. At a young age I learned that you own labels by defying them, and defy them by owning them. I know that the final word on me will be one that I choose.

Seventy-seven of those unseen soccer goals came courtesy of my head, and I am often asked to explain the technique: how my body knew where to be and how high to leap, how I sensed and facilitated the connection with the ball. For me, soccer was, and is, an intricate, chaotic dance, one that demands the repetition and mastery of its steps. In every game, in every play, my chance of scoring was directly proportionate to my recollection of previous goals. From past experience, I could predict the trajectory of the ball and position my head to meet it, finding the sweet spot just before everything went dark.

Soccer has taught me many lessons, but the greatest one is this: sometimes the only way to move forward is by first looking back.

2

TOMBOY

I am five years old, my legs pinwheeling across a soccer field, guiding the ball with my tiny cleats. My mouth is dry from catching the wind. I have only played the game a few times, but it already feels familiar, a task my body knows how to execute without much effort or direction, as though I'd been moving this way since the womb. The ball seems to be magnetically attached to my feet as I push past and through my opponents, looking for my mother in the stands, watching her watch me. When I am on the field I am her sole focus; I imagine myself as something so shiny and special she's unable to look away.

Afterward she hugs me and tells me she's proud—of my effort, my ability, my dedication. Silently I replay her words and will her to repeat them. Then she hesitates, curls her hands over my shoulders, and lowers herself to my level.

"Abby," she says, "you scored a lot of goals today. Don't you think it's important that your teammates become part of it?"

I look up at her, confused, and ask, "Isn't the whole point to score goals?"

She thinks on that for a moment and admits, "It is."

"Well, I am the best one to do that. So if that's the whole point, I don't see the problem."

She laughs, trapped by my innocent logic, and I'm not able to articulate my next thought: *If you weren't there to witness it, I wouldn't care about scoring at all.*

My six siblings and I are raised on competition. Tales of diligence and fortitude and success are passed down like cherished heirlooms. We hear about my great-grandfather, who bought a wooden stand, piled it high with colorful pyramids of fruit, and waved down each wagon passing through upstate New York. My grandfather improved upon the idea, trading in the wooden stand for a building and twenty-two acres of land, branding the business Wambach Farms. When he died he left everything to his only child, my father, who, upon his high school graduation, began working at the store seven days a week and has barely stopped since.

My father pauses long enough for dinner, coming home at 6 P.M. sharp before heading straight back to the store. His nightly presence at the table is one of the official family rules, a list curated and lengthened by my mother over the years. Another rule is the mandatory head count, instituted after my brother Pat was accidentally left home alone, Macaulay Culkin style, during an outing to a local restaurant.

Even manners are a contest. It is widely acknowledged that the Wambach kids are the nicest and best behaved in all of Pittsford, a conservative, suburban community just outside of Rochester. Pittsford is heavily Catholic and affluent, and we not only adhere to but improve on its unspoken code. It is mandated that we will be unfailingly polite to neighbors, strangers, and elders: we will send handwritten thank-you notes; we will hold open doors; we will not mouth off or cuss. We will attend Mass at St. Louis every Sunday, dressed in our finest, and sit erect in the front pew. “That priest up there?” my mom whispers. “He’s watching your every move. God is watching, too, so no monkey business.” We will behave when my parents go on their annual vacation to Florida, leaving us with our grandparents, occasionally for months at a time since my dad’s work was seasonal. We will listen. We will obey.

We will understand and acknowledge how blessed we are, and be exposed to those less fortunate. Every year, my parents enroll in the Fresh Air program, inviting city kids to stay with us for the summer. I look forward to these visits, eager for a glimpse of anything and anyone outside of my daily life. A boy named Manny is a repeat guest and I am obsessed with his hair, circling my hand atop his head as we sit and watch TV. When my mother bathes him he splashes and flails, protesting that she's trying to turn him white. On some level, I sense that I am different, too—a difference that stretches beyond my usual abilities on the soccer field. I know it will take time to understand how and why.

My mother's most cherished rule: there will be order and calm at the dinner table. Designated family time is sacrosanct. We are to share something about our day, one child at a time. My mother enforces this rule—and every rule—with what we all call "The Look": eyebrows pressed into a V, lips flattened into a line. The Look renders her invincible, a tyrant in Talbots and a conversion van. Being on the receiving end of it is punishment enough.

She turns her face toward me, the equivalent of being handed the conch in *Lord of the Flies*. I feel the glorious weight of everyone's attention, and I look at them one by one. My mother, who named me "Mary Abigail" after the Virgin Mary, and who has been dressing me in ruffles and bows since the day I was born. My father, who'd been a gifted athlete himself, wrestling and running track and playing football. My four brothers, who—at my request—take me to the neighborhood cul-de-sac, swaddle me in goalie pads, and crush slap shots at me until sundown. Soon, they will all dutifully begin working at the family store. My sister Laura: creative, free spirited, musically gifted. The oldest sibling, my sister Beth: athletic, brilliant, on her way to becoming an Ivy League–educated doctor. She's my second mother, always willing to tend to me when the real one runs out of time. After she leaves for college I become so sullen and withdrawn that my parents take me to a psychiatrist. "Being gone seems the same as being dead," I explain—an early lesson in the power of choosing to leave, and one that I will draw upon in the decades to come.

I pause, a forkful of mashed potatoes hovering by my mouth. I am beginning to realize that soccer is my secret weapon, the wand I can wave to invoke adoration and respect.

My father prods me. "How many goals did you score today, Abby?"

I beam at him. "A hat trick," I say. Three goals.

His response is swift: "Why not four?"

I have no answer. My mother shifts her face, passing the conch to my sister, and there is nothing I want more than to have another turn.

I score more hat tricks. I score more times than I can count. I score twenty-seven goals in three games and, at age nine, am sent to join the boys' league. They tease me, calling me "tomboy" and telling me to go back to the girls. I welcome this treatment and yearn to prove that I belong. I play football with my brothers and their friends, tackling one neighborhood kid so brutally I leave him moaning on the ground. I add basketball to my schedule and discover that it helps my soccer game; I become an amateur kineticist, analyzing how bodies leap and lean to meet rebounding balls. During my weekly phone call with Beth—established so I'm reassured that she's still alive—she asks if I won my latest basketball game.

"Sure did," I reply. "Thirty-two to nothing."

"That's great! How many points did you score?"

"Thirty-two."

I apply my newfound knowledge to the soccer field, experimenting with headers, taking note of how the ball launches from my forehead. My father, ever the pragmatist, orders me to move from central midfielder to forward, since the latter position guarantees more opportunities to score. In eighth grade, I am recruited to start on the varsity team for Our Lady of Mercy High School, the private, all-girls' institution that my sisters attended. I start participating in the Olympic Development Program (ODP), which gives me exposure to college and national team coaches. I grant my first interview to a local television station.

"Where do you get your athletic prowess?" the reporter asks.

"My mom played zero sports," I say. "But my dad was one of the fastest white runners in New York State."

Only later do I realize that those words might cause offense.

With each passing day soccer carves a larger scoop of my life. I love it for what it gives me: praise, affection, and, above all, attention. When I'm on the field I don't have to plead to be noticed, either silently or aloud; it is a natural by-product of my talent. I loathe it for the same reason, terrified that soccer is the only worthwhile thing about me, that stripping it from my identity might make me disappear. My future teammate and friend Mia Hamm will one day offer this advice: "Somewhere behind the athlete you've become and the hours of practice and the coaches who have pushed you is a little girl who fell in love with the game and never looked back . . . play for her."

I am not, and never will be, that little girl. Already I know I'm incapable of falling in love with the game itself—only with the validation that comes from mastering it, from bending it to my will.

I hate soccer even more when my mother declares that I must forgo my vacation at Stella Maris, the Catholic summer camp I've attended for as long as I can remember. My heart deflates. I am fourteen and not yet ready to let go of being a kid. It is the one place where I can do crafts and play tetherball and exist without any obligation to soccer. Instead, she says, I will have to go to soccer camp and work on improving my technique.

This is not the first time our philosophies have diverged. A part of me holds residual anger about her long trips to Florida. *You come back and now you want to be my mom?* I seethe silently. *You haven't been here!* To her alarm, I am now refusing to wear dresses, even to church. On Sunday morning I pull on sweatpants, sending her into apoplectic panic. I know I'm inviting The Look, and she delivers it on cue, a disapproval so potent it heats the air around us. But I dig in, refusing to budge. I might have inherited a sports gene from my father, but my obstinacy comes solely from her. The strategy works brilliantly as a bargaining tool, as a means of finding middle ground, and when I slide into the front pew I'm wearing pants and a shirt. She blames my behavior on a desire to be like my brothers, and I want to tell her, *No, this is all me*. I want her to love me anyway.

But with soccer, I fear there's no compromising.

"Mom," I plead, "I need to learn life. And I need to learn life through my mistakes, too. My life can't be all your choices. If I make a mistake I want it to be *my* mistake."

A persuasive argument, I think, but my mother remains unmoved.

I huff off to sulk in my room but am stopped by my brother Andy on the stairs.

"I'm going to quit soccer," I announce.

He drops his hand on my arm, holding me still, and speaks to me in a tone I've never heard.

"You have such a gift," he says. "You have to accept that. You can't quit. You would be doing all of us a disservice. We all wish we had half of your talent."

I feel as though I'm being asked to choose between soccer and myself, and I'm not sure how—or even if—one can exist without the other. I'm determined to have both.

I acquiesce and spend my summer at soccer camp, all the while plotting other ways to rebel.

3

REBEL

My revolt comes in increments, tiptoeing around the periphery of soccer without attacking it directly. I am playing five days a week for Mercy High School, two games and three practices, and I challenge my body to see how much abuse it can withstand. Every morning on the drive to school, I steer my hand-me-down Chevy into McDonald's for a breakfast sandwich and a Coke, the first of at least a dozen sodas I'll drink that day. On a dare I devour an entire stick of butter. I scarf large orders of chicken wings, then hold the box aloft to drink every drop of grease that's pooled at the bottom. Before practice I eat fifteen fried pizza rolls and then run a timed mile, vomiting as soon as I hit the finish line. I ride a Jet Ski straight into a lightning storm. I smoke pot and discover

I can drink copious amounts of beer. When my parents are in Florida I throw a sixteenth-birthday party for Audrey, my friend and teammate, and hold her hair when she's sick. "All I remember is that your sink is made by Delta," she tells me the next morning, and from then on every drinking binge is designated a "Delta Night."

I am the only child my mother doesn't trust, a fact she shares openly and often. None of my brothers or sisters ever had a curfew, but mine is 11 P.M., a full hour before my friends have to be home. If I pull into the driveway at 10:45, I sit there and wait so I'm not a second early. Once, while she's in Florida, I get my tongue pierced. As I leave for school, she plants herself between me and the door.

"You have a tongue ring," she says. "I want it out of your mouth and sitting on this table by 5 P.M. or I'm going to sue the pants off that place you went to."

I don't want to be on the news for my tongue ring, so I do as she asks, but our war turns more volatile with each successive round.

"I wish you were dead!" I scream at her, and she spins on her heel and orders me to her "office"—a small bathroom on our main floor. When she closes the door I expect The Look, but instead she is expressionless, all of her features fixed into place. She speaks with terrifying calmness and clarity: "One day when I *am* dead, you are going to regret saying that."

She closes the door and I imagine her reaction on the other side. *Oh, that got her,* I picture her whispering, and this time she's inarguably right.

My grades are horrendous. Instead of listening to lectures I practice my autograph, filling my notebooks with hundreds of ornate *Abby Wambach*s, picturing the lines of future fans. I realize my eyes focus differently, one nearsighted and the other far. This discrepancy helps my soccer game, allowing me to gauge the ball at every distance, but thwarts my attempts to read. My eyes fight each other for dominance, exhausting my brain. My book reports have nothing to do with the subject matter at hand. For *Pride and Prejudice* I might craft an essay on anthropomorphic lions; Orwell's *1984* inspires commentary about how differently he and I recall that particular year. My English teacher returns my work covered in bright red question marks.

"What book did you read?" she asks.

I shrug and respond, "That's what I got out of it."

I know I only have to do well enough to get into college, and that college will be paid for by a full sports scholarship. Soccer is unscathed by my bad behavior. On this front alone I heed my mother's wishes, listening to my coach, Ms. Boughton, and obeying her every order. In my sophomore year she makes me captain and motivates me with insults.

"Get on your horse!" she yells. "Stop being so goddamn lazy. You're not playing to your capability. You're not displaying the level of commitment a leader should have. I don't give a shit if you want to quit." I test this assertion, informing her routinely that I never want to play soccer again. Panicked, she calls my mother, who laughs and offers this advice: "Just give her time." To Coach Boughton's relief, my mother is right: in two weeks I'm back on the field, chasing the ball with my head.

No one has ever spoken to me like that in my life, and I gratefully internalize every word. I'm tired of hearing about my talent and am desperate to know my flaws; I want to corner and confront them and coax them into improvement. I want to be better, if only because being better ensures more attention. I am the last kid left in high school and now my mother has time to come to my games, chatting with the other parents in between blows of the whistle.

In my mind, her conversations are all about Beth: the smart one, the responsible one, the first great athlete of the family, who led Mercy's basketball team to a state championship. Beth's name, in fact, is emblazoned on a banner in the gym. In my mind, my mother's greatest question is whether I can win the championship, too, and the challenge blooms inside me, shading all of my thoughts. *If I win, maybe they'll love me the most. If I win, maybe I'll finally love myself.*

I have a boyfriend, my first, and he tells me he loves me all the time. His name is Teddy Barton and he plays soccer for McQuaid, the companion boys' school to Mercy. His older brother knew who I was and prompted him to ask me to a Jerry Garcia concert, and we've been together, off and on, ever since. The "off" times come when he becomes frustrated with my commitment to soccer; half of our dates involve him watching my games.

Teddy has dark eyes and long, shaggy brown hair that puts up in a ponytail. After soccer practice we drive his old-school BMW 5 series to his parents' house. He has the entire third floor to himself, and we are free to smoke cigarettes and drink beer and make out without fear of anyone barging in to stop us. My parents approve: he's a smart, athletic kid from a good family, with plans to become a naval pilot, one eye already looking toward the future. They even invite us to double-date with them at their country club, where they take pride in the fact that the servers and members all know my name.

We're the unofficial "jock couple" of Rochester. His friends become my friends—I can drink them under the table and outplay them on the field—and I pretend not to hear their jokes: *Teddy, your girlfriend is bigger than you are. Teddy, your girlfriend is gay.*

It's true, I am tall—I grew ten inches within a year and now measure five foot eleven—but I am not gay. At least I don't *think* I am, since I'm not sure what "gay" feels like, or how that identity would fit if I tried it on. On the walls of my room hang posters of the usual nineties heartthrobs, Brad Pitt and Tom Cruise and River Phoenix, and I wouldn't mind substituting Teddy for any of them. When he takes me to a Dave Matthews concert, the singer kisses me on the cheek and I refuse to let Teddy touch that spot for the rest of the night. I am still a tomboy, but no more so than any other female athlete at my school; we all wear backward baseball caps over our ponytails. I think I love Teddy, but then again, I am not sure what "love" feels like, either.

One Saturday night in my junior year, I am determined to get closer to an answer. Teddy tells me he has a surprise for me and picks me up early, explaining it's a bit of a drive to our destination. He's wearing pants and a stiffly starched shirt, a few steps up from his usual attire of ripped jeans and a tee, and he tells me I am beautiful; he especially loves my dimples when I smile.

It's about forty minutes to his family's cottage on Conesus Lake, and he holds my hand in between shifting the gears of his BMW. About halfway there it begins snowing; he slows down but won't turn back. The drive takes twice as long as it should, and when we arrive I see that he's already been there: a fire crackles, flowers burst from vases, and the pillows on the bed are conspicuously fluffed. He kisses me, and my clothes come off one piece at a time. The heat from the fire pricks my skin. He's on me now, feeling heavier than he really is, hurting me in a way he never has. I wonder, briefly, if we are doing it wrong, and then it's over before I can decide.

The more we experiment, the less it hurts. I begin to enjoy it, and I also appreciate the cover it provides me: no one can think I'm gay if I'm doing it with a boy.

On the night of his senior prom, my mom is pleased by the sight of me in a flouncy dress and heels, which do make me considerably taller than Teddy. We drink and dance and he begs me to stay out late, but I have a game the next day and need to be home by curfew. Within the week Audrey is on the phone, saying she has a hypothetical question.

"What if you knew your best friend's boyfriend cheated on her?" she asks. "Would you tell her?"

"When did Teddy cheat on me?" I reply, bluffing. A part of me doesn't think he's capable of it.

"Oh! I didn't think you'd figure that out."

"He did?" I ask. "When? Who?"

It was after I left prom, she says. A girl from a different school.

I ignore his repeated pleas for forgiveness and am surprised by my reaction: my pride is wounded more than my heart.

One day after soccer practice, my parents and I stop at the Macaroni Grill. I still remember my precise outfit at seventeen: white turtleneck, blue corduroy pants, Doc Martens, and a bright yellow North Face jacket I'd saved up to buy. Our server approaches, wearing a crisp white shirt and skinny tie. She's eighteen years old, has long brown hair and green eyes and seems to be smiling only at me.

I can't look directly at her. I can't look away. I *like* her. I like her in a way I have never liked Teddy.

I don't remember ordering, or what my parents talk about; their words coast over me, and there's a booming silence in my ears, and my heart lurches against my chest. Energy thrums through every limb; my feet tap and my fingers shake. When the server walks away to get our drinks, I pick up a crayon from the table's basket and doodle a soccer ball, willing myself to calm. I feel as though a switch has flipped inside me, blinking neon and illuminating my secrets for all the world to see.

When she comes back she's still smiling at me, and points at the soccer ball I scrawled on my placemat.

"Oh, you play soccer?" she asks.

"Yes, I play soccer."

"That's super cool. I played lacrosse and soccer."

I tell her I attend Mercy High School, and she asks if I know the famous soccer player who goes there, the girl who is always on the local news.

"I know her," I admit. "That's me."

I learn her name is Stephanie, and when she clears our plates her hand skims the length of my pinky finger, a touch all the more powerful in its brevity. I need to feel it again, and I want to understand that need.

Silently I repeat the three syllables of her name all the way home.

I pace in my room, back and forth between my window and my door. *What was that?* I don't know what to do with the feeling, which has already taken root in my psyche, robust and resolute. For a moment I wonder if it's just my latest attempt to rebel, and in a way I know will hurt my mother the most. I'm a bad Catholic, a sexual deviant on my way straight to hell—where, in my private version, I will have to play soccer in an empty stadium for all of eternity.

This feeling is worth the risk. I sit down at my desk and type a letter, picking my words with care:

Dear Stephanie,

I was one of your clients today, and we got to talking. I can't really tell you who I am, and I don't know what this feeling is about, but I want to get to know you. I've never done this before. If you know who this is, look me up in the phone book and please call me.

Without knocking, my brother Andy barrels into my room.

"Get out!" I yell. "I'm doing something personal." Hunching over the letter, I turn my face just enough to scowl at him.

He's curious, I can tell, but he backs away.

I mail it to "Stephanie, c/o the Macaroni Grill."

I wait, and hold my breath with each ring of the phone. On the third day she's on the other line.

"Hey!" she says. "This is Stephanie from the Macaroni Grill."

"Cool," I say, trying to steady my voice. "How are you?"

"Well, I got this letter. And I wondered if the letter was from you."

"A letter?" I act surprised. "What letter?"

"Oh, you didn't send a letter to the Macaroni Grill? My bad, so sorry."

I laugh and tell her I was just fucking with her, and it was me. It *is* me. And I know that whatever this feeling is, she has it, too.

We begin to see each other feverishly, discreetly. I tell no one, but a group of Goth girls recognize my covert identity; one morning I find a rainbow sticker slapped to the back of my Chevy Blazer, and I scrape every last strip of it off. I go to great lengths to hide my relationship from my teammates and friends. Once, on the way back from a soccer game in Syracuse, I detour to Stephanie's house and lose all track of time, missing both family dinner and curfew. My mom calls Audrey's house to ask if she knows where I am. For once, she doesn't. Neither does my friend Breaca, who later is offended that I unnecessarily kept my secret from her. When I get home I concoct a plausible explanation, and if my mother doesn't believe me she keeps it to herself.

I was just as terrible a liar back then.

Throughout senior year I hear daily from college coaches who want me to play for them. They boast about their program, their campus, their vibrant social scene; some jokingly promise half of their salary. My mother gleefully stuffs a binder with offer letters and brochures. I visit four schools in quick succession—the University of North Carolina, George Mason, the University of Virginia, and UCLA—and am convinced I should choose the most geographically distant locale. "I'm done," I tell my mother. "I'm going to California. UCLA it is."

"No," she says, offering a modified version of The Look. "I'm trying to honor the fact that you want to make this decision, but you have to take five visits. The reason you don't want to go on one more visit is because you're lazy."

"Fine," I concede. "It's between Clemson or Florida, whoever calls first."

Slyly, without saying a word, my mother intervenes. She decides that Clemson is "too southern," and that, if I choose Florida, she and my father will be able to attend games when they're vacationing at their condo. She calls Florida's coach,

Becky Burleigh, advises her to hurry to seal the deal, and I'm off to visit Florida within the week.

The university's soccer program is brand new, a by-product of Title IX, the law that forbids any federally funded school to discriminate on the basis of sex, including in the creation and development of sports programs. Later, I'll realize how fortunate I was to have benefited from the law, which enabled American women's soccer to dominate on the international stage; FIFA estimates that 12 percent of youth soccer players are girls, and U.S. players comprise more than half that number. During the nearly four decades from 1941 to 1979, women in Brazil were completely barred from playing soccer. Even today, there's a stigma against Brazilian female players, who are sometimes called *sapatão,* a lesbian slur.

But now, as a seventeen-year-old high school senior, I'm not focused on the politics of soccer. I just like the idea of building something from the ground up, of being the underdog with something to prove. It's settled: I'll be playing for the Florida Gators. My mother wins the game without my knowing we were playing one.

I'm away on an ODP trip when I make the decision, and my mother helps me orchestrate my announcement. She lines up sweatshirts from all five prospective schools along the kitchen counter and summons reporters to the house. At the appointed time, I call home and tell my mother what she already knows. As she raises the Florida sweatshirt—number four in the lineup—over her head, everyone cheers and claps. "I'm going to a movie now," I tell her, knowing she's reveling in the spectacle.

In the waning months of my high school career I have just two things on my mind: the state championship and Stephanie. I know our relationship will likely end once I head to college, so I see her as much as possible, sometimes to the detriment of soccer. During an away game for the U.S. women's national Under-18 team, I play poorly on purpose, missing headers and tripping over my feet and letting opponents slip past. When the coach questions me I have a ready lie: my beloved uncle is hovering near death, and I really need to go home. I have one prepared for my parents, too: my ankle hurts, and I don't want to begin my college career as a liability for my team, so I must come home and rest. As soon as I'm there I find Stephanie. We are still the only ones privy to each other's secret, and I know that soon enough I will have to say it out loud.

She is there, watching, on the day Mercy High School plays Massapequa for the state championship. More than playing for the U-18 team, more than earning a full ride to college, more, even, than identifying my sexuality, I see a state title as the pinnacle of my high school life. Winning will put my name up on a banner in the school auditorium, above my sister Beth's. Winning will correct my faults and fill in my gaps. It will make my mother see past all the parts of me she wishes she could change, including the parts she doesn't yet know.

Before the game the entire team congregates in the locker room, listening to our coach conduct what she calls an "imagery drill." We are to sit still and visualize how we'd like the game to unfold: picture the ball coming to you, and now you're racing down the sideline, and now you're crossing the ball up into the air, and now you're heading it into the goal. When we finish we form a circle, hands clasping shoulders, scalps touching. Silently I acknowledge that my performance will determine the outcome; one mistake and the loss will be something I have to own alone.

We play on field turf after a snowstorm, with a layer of slush still coating the ground. For the first sixty minutes the game progresses perfectly, as though I'd choreographed every move. I am playing better than I ever have, the ball kissing my forehead before it finds the net, and we are up 3–0 with twenty minutes left. Coach Boughton pulls me aside and tells me to play defense, and in my mind I think that's crazy—playing not to lose instead of to win—but I do what my mother would want me to do, and obey.

The minutes tick by: nineteen, eighteen, seventeen. Massapequa scores three goals in fast succession, and for the first time in my life the game slips away from me, operating on some plane I can't reach. I see their winning shot with cruel clarity, soaring past me, past all of us, the scoreboard lighting up to confirm our defeat. My defeat.

I sense myself growing smaller, my body curling inward, my elbows to my thighs, my head to my hands, my ponytail grazing the ground. I feel the sting of snow through my stockings, numbing the points of my knees. I am wailing, making a noise I have never heard, and it occurs to me that I have never before cried in public; I am terrified at the thought that my emotions might be recorded and judged. I don't know how long I'm there before my teammates surround me, hoisting me up an inch at a time. My legs feel detached, moving without orders from my brain, and they take me to the fence, where I see my mother waiting, her body stretching out to meet me. She pulls me in close, her hands touching behind my back, and fits her mouth to my ear: *I love you, Abby,* she says. *I love you.*

I relax against her, finally believing those words and feeling as though I've earned them. Seventeen years later, when I am retired and alone in my hotel room, the days slurring past without much direction or hope, it is one of the memories that sustains me.

4

TEAMMATE

On the night before I leave for college, I sit with friends on my front steps until sunrise, sipping beer from Coke cans and finding shapes in the stars. I am eager to leave Pittsford, with its strict parameters and provincial expectations, with its ingrained expectations of who I am. For all of my eighteen years I've lived someone else's version of me, and I need to create a new model—one I recognize when I look in the mirror, one whose skin lies smoothly on my bones.

"Tomorrow a whole new life starts for me," I whisper. "I don't know when I'll come home again."

It's a prophetic thought: for the next eighteen years—the amount of time I've already been alive—I won't be in one place for longer than a month. I remember the lyrics I quoted on my yearbook page, from the October Project song "Ariel": *The day is breaking now. It's time to go away. I'm so afraid to leave, but more afraid to stay.*

I am ready to see what's next.

My mother has packed up nearly everything I own, leaving only my trophies behind, arranging each box in my new Jeep Wrangler with such tight precision that not an inch is wasted. My father struck a deal: if I got a full scholarship to college, he'd buy me the car of my choice. He angled for a BMW but I insisted on the Jeep, fearing judgments about arriving on campus in such an ostentatious car. He's also offered to pay fifty dollars for every college goal I score, a significant raise from my high school rate of twenty-five dollars. They follow me on the nineteen-hour drive down to Gainesville, making sure we're never separated by more than one car. I am exhausted from my late night, and a few hours into the drive I'm nodding off, swerving in and out of my lane. Insistent honking stirs me awake, and through my rearview mirror I see my mother waving her arms, flagging me to the side of the road. For the rest of the way we take turns, one of my parents driving my Jeep while I sprawl out on the passenger seat and close my eyes. My mother lowers the volume on the radio and shifts into fifth gear, working the stick with surprising ease. *Wow, when did Mom learn how to drive a stick shift?* I think, and I'm intrigued by the idea that she has secrets of her own.

A few days later, at 5 A.M., I show up at my first preseason practice wholly unprepared. Over the summer Coach Burleigh had sent a packet detailing how we should condition ourselves, but I refused to put down the Coke and beer and junk food, let alone go for a run. My teammates and I gather at one end of the field and wait for the shriek of the whistle. If I don't pass this fitness test, I won't be allowed to play. But I am used to abusing my body without repercussions; it has never failed to do what I tell it to do.

And I'm off: eight hundred yards in three minutes, around the track. I'm running swiftly, surprisingly fast for a big girl, finding my rhythm. Two minutes to rest and I'm only vaguely out of breath. Next up: a back-and-forth suicide run—six, eighteen, and sixty yards—in thirty-four seconds. Halfway through and I can hear my mother's voice: *I told you to go for a run, Abby. I warned you this would happen.* The sun grows hotter with each inch it ascends, battering my scalp. A veil of sweat clouds my eyes. During the forty-five-second rest I inhale air so greedily it scythes a path down my throat. *Oh my god, I can't do this,* I think, and then I'm off again, running four hundred yards in 1:25, both painfully present in my body and feeling as though I'm floating above it, a hapless witness to my own voluntary torture. I gulp only three hoarse breaths during the forty-five-second rest, and I order my legs to run again. Another 6–18–60 suicide, and my body begins to revolt, remnants of my last meal inching their way up my throat.

And then a dreadful realization: it is only half over.

I don't know how I can do it, I *can't* do it, I am physically incapable of running another step or taking another breath or stooping to graze the ground with my fingers, and then my body does something it never has before—it seizes control and speaks to my brain: *I am not going to stop, even if you think I'm finished. You have so much anger inside of you, layers and layers of rage, each a different flavor. Feeling like a failure, feeling like a freak, feeling abandoned and unloved and unlovable, feeling like an "athlete" is your only authentic identity, a sum total far greater than all of your parts. Take that anger and use it now to make me move.*

My mind submits to my body and my body responds in kind; for once there is accord between them. I am gaining speed, overriding every scream and aching bone, feeling possessed by a demon I freely invited inside. Another four hundred in 1:25, another 6–18–60 suicide, another eight hundred in 3:15. Through those last eight hundred yards I vomit and piss myself the entire way, but still my mind feeds its anger to my body and my body absorbs it all, using every last watt of energy until they both, at once, order me to stop. It's finished. I did it.

I think I might die. I have never felt so alive in my whole life. I hide under my towel, fearful that if I look up to watch the goalkeepers I might never be able to step on a field again—and I have to, in just a few hours, for more drills and a scrimmage. One of my new teammates, Heather Mitts, sits next to me. I lift the edge of my towel to peer up at her. She's a junior, two years older, with shiny blond hair and legs up to her armpits, and I suspect—correctly—that one day we'll be together on the U.S. national team.

"I don't know if I can do this," I confess.

She smiles, a quick flash of blindingly white teeth, and says, "Yeah, you can."

It's a dare as much as an order, and I believe I can comply—as long as my body and mind are speaking to each other.

Our team has twelve seniors, all of whom have been here from the beginning, when the program first launched four years ago. They become my surrogate family, substitutes for the older siblings I've left back north, and I am equally desperate to please them. My pedigree—142 high school goals, one of the country's top ten recruits, named the high school player of the year by numerous organizations—is irrelevant on my new field. Unlike at Mercy, this team doesn't depend solely on me. Raw talent is no longer enough, and I need to prove I belong on this field.

Every hellish three-a-day, every scrimmage, every game is a chance to seize their attention. I score on a header in my very first game, a 3–0 victory. I credit my goals to teammates, insisting that without their skillful serves, I wouldn't score at all. At a game in Connecticut, a male spectator begins harassing a teammate who also happens to be gay. "Hey, twenty-eight!" he yells to me, referencing my number. "Is number eight your girlfriend?" I deliberately kick the ball into the stands, a searing line drive that nearly collides with his head;

he subsequently leaves her alone. I cheer everyone on as they run their suicides, sometimes literally pushing them across the finish line. I stay just fit enough to cross the line myself. *Look at me,* I think. *See me. Notice me. Love me—if not for who I am, then for what I can do.*

What I want to do, what we *all* want to do, is find our way to the NCAA tournament, where we will inevitably meet the University of North Carolina Tar Heels, who've won the championship game fourteen out of the last sixteen years. Every time we play the Tar Heels they dominate the field, beating us four times over the three previous years. I have my own personal vendetta against North Carolina—in particular, its legendary coach: Anson Dorrance was the only one who refused to offer me a full scholarship (he offered a partial, a gesture that, in my teenage memory, was downgraded to the cost of a couple of textbooks). The Tar Heels are a dynasty, a fearsome Goliath that churns out stars for the national team with assembly-line efficiency, and I am determined to play a role in knocking them down.

Early in our season it becomes clear that we have something; we *are* something, and we feel invincible in our cohesion. We beat teams the Gators had never beaten before: Southern Methodist University and Texas A&M and Vanderbilt, and as our first game against UNC approaches we see no reason for the streak to end. In October, in front of five thousand fans—including my parents, who attend every game—it does end, but barely. One of our seniors ties the game one-all in the eighty-sixth minute and forces extra time, during which the Tar Heels score. But this loss feels different, like it's halfway to a win. It is our only loss of the season, and we're hell-bent to meet the Tar Heels again.

We do, two months later, in Greensboro, North Carolina, just fifty miles away from UNC's home field. It's our first time in the NCAA championship tournament, and just one game stands between us and the national title. We are ready, and within the first six minutes our captain scores on a free kick, soaring the ball over the head of the Tar Heel goalkeeper and lighting up our side of the board. The next eighty-four minutes are some of the ugliest soccer I've ever played, a ferocious stretch of hustle and vigilance and hurling myself at the ball, all 170 pounds of me tumbling forward and coming to rest on my face. Every minute stretches interminably, and toward the end, at the final TV timeout, Coach Burleigh summons us together for a huddle. We sling slick arms around each other's necks and fidget, stabbing at the turf with our cleats.

I look at my teammates, one by one, as if I'm back home in Pittsford at the dinner table, waiting for my chance to talk. This is the seniors' time, their last shot, and I have been respectful of the team's hierarchy, being ready when they need me and stepping back when they don't. But no one is louder or more insistent than the youngest of seven, and I decide that they need me now, that some words are best said in my voice.

Rearing my head back, I roar: "We are not fucking losing to these bitches!"

When I lower my face I see everyone is looking at me. Coach Burleigh mentally discards whatever speech she's prepared and says, "Okay then. Let's go."

We run out, whooping and slapping palms, and when the final buzzer sounds my vulgar prophecy comes true: the score stays steady and we win. In that moment, buried beneath a pile of euphoric teammates, it's so easy to trust that my voice will never fail me.

5

LESBIAN

One night, at a house party, I debate how to tell my teammates that I'm gay. They suspect something, I'm sure of it; their whispers—not malicious, just curious—follow me into the locker room and to the bars after games. Once, after many rounds of beer, we start a drinking game: "Never have I ever." Everyone takes a turn: "Never have I ever . . . shoplifted." A few guilty parties take a swig. "Never have I ever . . . walked in on my parents having sex." One girl cringes at the memory and chugs, eliciting sympathetic pats on the back. I'm next. *Fuck it,* I think. *"Gay" is only one part of who you are, and you should be as vocal about that as you are about everything else.*

I hoist a can of Bud Light in the air and say, "Never have

I ever . . . kissed a girl!" Within seconds I drain the beer and, as an exclamation point, crush the can in my hand.

"I knew it!" they say, laughing, and move on to the next. I'm happy they accept me but I know I cheated the revelation, declaring my sexuality without actually saying the word.

I still have my long blond ponytail, a vestige of traditional femininity I can't yet bring myself to shed, and guys hit on me regularly. Early sophomore year, at an athletes' party, one approaches me, pressing a beer into my hand. He's imposing, six-two and about two hundred pounds, and he tells me his name is Are—spelled like the verb, but pronounced like the letters: R.E. For the next three hours, until every keg is kicked, we drink and talk and eventually conclude, with mutual delight, that we are the loudest, most obnoxious people in the room, and I think nothing of it when he accompanies me back to my dorm.

We tumble onto the bed, our huge bodies filling the mattress, and lie chastely side by side. He twists his face toward mine. I recognize that look and realize I should clarify my position before he gets the wrong idea.

"I need to tell you something," I say. "This isn't going where you seem to think it's going. I like girls."

"That's cool," he replies, and from then on we are inseparable.

I decide Are is me, exactly, in a slightly bigger body. He is my wingman as I negotiate my first "out" adult relationships. At a party early my sophomore year, I spot a girl with long dark hair and lithe, sleek limbs standing quietly in the corner. Her name is Nikki and she's a nationally ranked tennis player. She knows all too well the pressure of being forced to perform, the feeling of hating the very thing that brings you love. We connect over our mutual determination to have a life outside of our sport, to be more than who we are on the court and the field. She is three years older than I, inching closer to deciding what she wants to do with her life, and before long I'm hoping, with terrifying intensity, that those plans will always include me.

Our relationship reminds me that I need to tend to my life outside of soccer, and Are is a willing accomplice. When I'm not with Nikki or on the field, he and I are sitting in my dorm room playing video games and smoking pot and dipping Kodiak chewing tobacco, a nasty habit that develops into a lifelong vice. He is as competitive as I am and always up for a drinking contest. At Balls, our favorite campus bar, we shotgun one beer after another, punching a hole into the bottom of the can and swallowing its contents within seconds. The next day, on the field, I talk my body into performing and it complies with herculean resilience. During one game, I defy my hangover to execute what I still consider the best goal of my career, diving facedown and curling my legs in the air, scorpion style, kicking the ball in with my heels.

I rationalize that I am not hurting my game, but rather helping it. My astrological sign is Gemini, and I have true twin personalities, always at odds with each other. On my right shoulder perches responsible, dedicated Intense Abby, serious about honing her technique and maintaining her fitness, always cognizant of her growing role as a leader on the team. On the left, whispering loud enough to fill both ears, is bad, rebellious Chill Abby, who argues, with skillful conviction, that if she lets soccer supplant every aspect of her being, she will not be able to play at all.

Despite Chill Abby's triumphs, my game remains intact and the honors accumulate: two-time SEC Player of the Year, two-time SEC Tournament Most Valuable Player, first-team All-American three years in a row. I'm on my way to setting a school record for goals, assists, game-winning goals, and hat tricks, and the national team coaches are taking notice. During spring of my junior year I'm selected to attend camp in California for the U.S. Under-21 team. There we scrimmage against teams from America's first women's professional league, the Women's United Soccer Association (WUSA). At the end of camp I'm summoned to confer with Jerry Smith, the U-21 coach and the husband of Brandi Chastain, one of the stars of the 1999 World Cup–winning women's team.

I bound into Jerry's office, eager for his assessment.

"How do you think you did?" he asks.

"Well," I say, "I scored the most goals."

He nods. "That's the hardest thing to do. How did the rest of your game go?"

There's a strange lilt to his voice, as if it's a trick question, and I hesitate before I respond. "What do you think?"

"Terribly," he says. "You do the hardest thing to do in our

sport better than anyone else here, but the rest of your game has a long, long way to go. You're unfit, you're a defensive liability, and you're only good at attacking when you're in a scoring position. There's so much more to the game, and if you want to stay with us you'll have to bust your butt or I won't bring you back to camp. In fact, I'm not bringing you to the next camp. You have talent and I would love to invest in you, but you have to have more skin in the game."

I'm quiet, considering his words. I long for criticism, and yet I'm reluctant to commit to what it asks of me.

"Is this meeting over?" I ask, finally.

"That's it," he says, and motions toward the door.

One month later, back in Gainesville, I send Jerry an e-mail. "I thought about what you said," I write, "and it has had an impact on me. If you bring me back, I'll show you."

He responds immediately: he was hoping to hear exactly that.

I implore Intense Abby to be patient while Chill Abby celebrates her twenty-first birthday: a drink for every year I've been alive, with Are and Nikki by my side.

These days, my relationship with Nikki is as exhausting as consecutive suicide runs. She's graduated and now lives in New York City, and we take turns dating long-distance and calling it off altogether. I am still insanely in love with her and desperate to make it work, but she is hesitant, both about me and about her sexuality. I'm the first girl she's dated, and the needle is still wavering on her Kinsey scale. I send her love letters and gifts and offer to watch her dog, but I will never pressure her to come out to her family; I am not even out to mine.

Intense Abby steps in and argues that hard work and focus will be a worthy distraction from my romantic troubles. At the insistence of Coach Burleigh, who fears my lackadaisical fitness might ruin my prospects with the national team, I make an appointment with Randy Brauer, a muscular therapist who trains the Gators football players. We meet by the track, and Randy tells me to run, observing me from the sidelines. After one lap he holds up a hand, halting me.

"Good god," he says. "Has anyone ever taught you how to run? You're leaving craters in the track." Not only are my feet improperly positioned, but my body is tightly coiled: fists clenched, brows furrowed, mouth pursed, shoulders raised to my ears. I need to relax and stop fighting myself. Intense Abby is nothing if not coachable, and within two weeks my steps are nearly imperceptible, quicker and lighter than they've ever been.

I test them one day during a training session. One of Randy's athletes, a starring center for the football team, makes a comment as I sprint past. I don't recall what he said but I'll never forget his tone, the snide veneer coating his words. I interpret the tone as judgment. Years later, when I am wholly comfortable in my skin, I will be judged in similar ways—questioning looks when I walk into bathrooms or through airport security, looks that require me to cinch my voice an octave higher to say "Hi," and, if that fails, to declare, bluntly,

"I am a *girl*." It will happen so often, for so long, that it will become a joke to me and my teammates, yet a part of me will always find it hurtful, and want people to pay better attention, to take the time to look. To *see* me.

But in college, such comments, purposeful or otherwise, are not funny at all. Standing on that track, I remember how far I have come and shrink at how far I have to go. Right then, straddling the middle, I am not in the mood to be judged.

The football player is a big boy, three hundred pounds, and could easily bench-press twice his weight. I hear a silent whistle and I'm off, scorching the field with my feet, running at him with all I have, as if each step might be my last. He's on bended knee, studying his foot, and doesn't even hear me coming until I'm on top of him, knocking him over and belly-flopping onto his chest. I am near feral, teeth bared, kicking and growling as we flip and fumble across the grass, and when he finally escapes, scrabbling away, I rise up and think: *Victory*.

I take a step closer to becoming myself, fully and without reservation. Are is looming behind me, an electric razor poised at my scalp. "Do it," I order, and he does. My hair drops in long blond sheaths, forming a shag carpet on his floor. Are's mother, Dena, stands to the side wielding tweezers. "You gotta fucking teach me to pluck my eyebrows," I tell her, and she obliges, starting on the left. "Ow! Ow! Ow!" As she pinches and pulls, I force myself to ask her a question: "What would you do if your kid was gay?"

She withdraws the tweezers and catches my reflection in the mirror. "I would just hope they could find love and happiness," she says.

Smiling, I motion for her to finish.

The next day, Are and Dena sit next to my parents at my game. My mother gasps when she sees me. "Oh my gosh," she says, elbowing my father. "Peter! I cannot even believe that's Abby's head. Oh my gosh. This is a tragedy!"

"A tragedy is the Twin Towers coming down," Are points out, "not Abby's haircut."

The shock of my hairstyle is eclipsed by the news that I won't be graduating. With just a few months left of school, I'm drafted by the Washington Freedom for the WUSA's second season. My parents help me pack up my life in Florida and move to an apartment on the outskirts of Washington, D.C. When the last box is emptied, my father hands me a credit card bill showing eight thousand dollars in charges. My mother stands nearby, watching him.

"What's this?" I ask.

"A bill for your partying," he says. "Did you really think I was going to pay for four years of your partying?"

I smile, attempting levity. "Well, yeah."

"I've been paying the minimum for four years—you can take it over now."

I take the bill and think, *You have no control over me anymore. No one does.*

Next time, my mother comes to visit me alone. I take her to lunch at Chevy's, a Mexican place near Pentagon City. I'm sweating, the heat of my hands defrosting my chilled glass. She sips her iced tea and scans the menu. My heart thumps in time with the mariachi music. I can tackle a massive bear of a football player without hesitation, but I am deathly afraid of this woman. When I find my voice, it squeaks into the air an octave higher than usual, and I feel like I'm back in Pittsford, fighting against wearing dresses and weathering The Look.

"Mom," I say, and pause. "I've got to tell you something. I've been meaning to do this for a long time. I'm nervous, and I'm really sorry if this upsets you, but I'm a lesbian."

Her reaction is swift and unexpected. "No, you're not," she says, pursing her lips.

My body straightens in the booth. "Yeah, I am."

"Abby, no, you're not."

"Yeah, I am."

She shakes her head. "Abby, you just don't know what it's like to be with a guy."

I understand: in some deep, secluded corner of her mind I am still a good and proper Catholic, virginal, waiting for marriage.

"Mom," I say softly. "If you're talking about sex, I do know what it's like to have sex with a guy . . . I'm dating someone, a woman. I've dated a few girls. I dated Teddy, remember, and I'm much happier dating girls."

Her expression is one of stern sadness, as though she's caught between recognition and resignation. She opens and closes her mouth, debating her next words, and then she gives herself permission to say them: "Don't tell me you have one of those strappy things."

I drain a full glass of water while I contemplate how to respond.

"Mom," I say, "do you ask any of your other children about their sexual behaviors behind closed doors?"

"No," she admits.

"Do you want to start now?"

"No."

"Okay," I say.

We order and eat, and for once in my life I don't know how to fill the silence.

6

ROOKIE

Every day I wake up and repeat my mantra: *No one controls me anymore.* I make my own money now, around thirty thousand dollars per year, an amount that, to my twenty-two-year-old self, seems inconceivable. I buy a motorcycle, a chili-pepper-red crotch rocket that I zip around the streets of Georgetown. I make a few unfortunate fashion choices, growing my hair into a haphazard mullet and wearing a leopard-print cowboy hat. I am still on-and-off with Nikki, and she is still not out to her family; I understand but am slowly losing patience. I want a commitment, a plan. I want a future.

I crave some vestige of comfort and familiarity, so I invite my old high school friend Audrey to live with me. Chill

Abby and Intense Abby are in balance, neither one overpowering the other. Chill Abby still eats and drinks whatever she wants, but Intense Abby is determined to excel at her new job with the Washington Freedom, to keep getting called to the national roster. No one controls me anymore, but the knowledge still burrows in my brain: If I play well, my mother might forgive me for being who I am. If I play well, I might forgive her for wishing I were someone else.

Nevertheless, I am growing more brazen about my sexuality, and come out to my Washington Freedom teammates without any reservations. One morning, en route to a game, our driver takes a wrong turn. "We're going to have to flip a bitch," someone says, a euphemism for making a U-turn. "Well, *I'll* flip a bitch," I quip, and am relieved when everyone laughs.

The star of the Washington Freedom is Mia Hamm, member of the legendary '99 World Cup–winning team and the most famous female soccer player in the country. Back in Pittsford, in my childhood bedroom, a signed poster of her occupies a place of honor over my bed. Mia's popularity is the prime reason the WUSA exists at all. She is eight years older than I, six inches shorter, forty pounds lighter, several decibels quieter, and infinitely more terrifying than she appears. Last year, during my official debut for the national team, I was called off the bench as a late substitute in an exhibition game against Germany. For the entire eighteen minutes I played Mia yelled at me—Where was I going? Why wasn't I moving? What the hell was I doing?—and she approached me afterward, explaining that she knew I was tough enough to take it.

Before our season begins, Mia has arthroscopic surgery on her left knee and is projected to miss the first ten games. Nevertheless she's at every practice and match, screaming from the sidelines, and whenever I exit the field she suggests ways I can improve. I'm leaning too far back when I shoot, she says, and that's why the ball is going over the bar. I need to remember to drop my shoulder. I should use my big body as often as I can. I still covet criticism over praise, and absorb everything she says. At season's end, I'm named the WUSA's Rookie of the Year.

Tacitly, subconsciously, that honor signals that I can coast a bit, relax into my vices. Chill Abby takes a step forward, positioning herself as my dominant personality. I party just a bit harder than I play and my body regresses, forgetting how it moves at its peak. April Heinrichs, the coach of the women's national team, begins excluding me from important games. One night she pulls me aside and renders a verdict I've heard before: I'm unfit, I'm lazy, I'm uncompetitive. If I don't shape up, and quickly, I won't be playing with the women's national team. I'll miss the 2003 World Cup, my first.

I listen; I focus; I push Chill Abby away. I finish my second season with the Washington Freedom with a league-leading thirty-three goals, including the winner at the championship game—the "golden goal," it's called, since it happened in overtime. Our celebration is short-lived; three weeks later, on September 15, 2003, the WUSA folds. The 99ers are beloved, but their fame is not enough to sustain an eight-team league—especially when the target audience, teenage girls, have their own games to attend. I am out of a job and worried that we'll never be able to reignite that national passion for women's soccer, that our sport is destined to be less than, irrelevant, othered.

The World Cup was initially scheduled to be held in China, but after the SARS outbreak, it was moved to the U.S., and we were determined to take advantage of playing at home. Rides on the team bus are usually a raucous party, with my voice the loudest of them all; I channel my nervous energy into singing (badly), dancing (even worse), and chattering in nonsensical stream-of-consciousness monologues. Julie Foudy, another 99er and the captain of the national team, once gave me a T-shirt emblazoned with the words HELP! I'M TALKING AND I CAN'T SHUT UP. But this time the atmosphere on the bus is subdued, everyone weighing their private pressures and concerns.

Mia and Julie are hoping that a World Cup victory might revive the WUSA; if the team plays as it did in 1999, the sponsors could be persuaded to invest again. A few days earlier, I was profiled in the *New York Times,* with the headline calling me a "Mass of Woman" and the article positioning me as a potential breakout star for the team. Intense Abby is hyperaware of the expectations percolating all around—and within—her. I am the one major piece that's different from the '99 team, the new ingredient that remains untested and unknown.

We start with wins in our group: against Sweden, Nigeria, North Korea, Norway. Despite the victories, the crowds are small and subdued. People are preoccupied with football season; more than that, the ghost of the failed WUSA seems to haunt each stadium we play. On Sunday, October 5, we face Germany at PGE Park in Portland, Oregon, just a few miles from where I will one day live with my wife.

From the beginning the game feels off, a dance where the team is a half step behind. The day before, we had practiced set pieces, predicting how and where and when Germany would attack, but our opponents are not behaving as expected; then build-up is cautious and deliberate. I have a "mark," the player I'm supposed to defend (and, in Coach Heinrich's words, "run over like a Mack truck"). Her name is Kerstin Garefrekes and she is five-ten, just one inch shorter than I, but lighter and leaner; my body should overpower hers in any showdown. I have studied her play and asked my teammates about her history, and I believe I can anticipate her every dodge and step. But somehow, in the first fifteen minutes, she moves in a way I don't predict, positioning herself near post. On a corner kick, she finds the ball before I do and bangs her head against it, bouncing it off the crossbar and into the net. They score twice more, and we don't score at all.

No matter that my mark didn't make the game-winning goal; I allowed her to set the tone. That thought attacks me with every bit of strength I have, and a new mantra blooms inside my head: *This loss is your fault*. It is the high school state championship all over again, and I want to disappear, to rewind my life back to a time before I ever pulled on cleats or headed a ball. Tonight, I will spend hours in the shower, wailing and weeping and beating my fists against the tile, but this time my grief will be private. Now, though, I force myself to stay on the field, watching my teammates cry while the Germans celebrate, climbing on each other's backs, chanting words I can't understand.

I feel an arm drop across my shoulders and hear Coach Heinrichs say, "Come on, let's go inside."

"No," I tell her, my eyes still fixed on the German team. "I want to remember this."

7

MANIC

For three weeks after the World Cup I can think of nothing but that first goal, the goal that spurred the Germans to a win, the goal I allowed. My mind replays the moment on a continuous loop, an excruciating image I'm powerless to block. Even the elements that were objectively out of my control become details in my narrative of failure: I should have known how my mark would pivot and spin. I should have beaten her to the ball. I should have hurled my body at her to throw her off balance. Somehow, magically, I should have rendered all the German players motionless through sheer force of will. I gnaw at myself with a quiet savagery. *My fault, my fault, my fault.*

I'm relieved when Coach Heinrichs announces the Olympic roster and I'm on the list. In February 2004, we start residency camp in Hermosa Beach, California, where I share an apartment with two teammates at 1212 Monterey Boulevard; we dub it "doce doce." I find solace in removing myself, geographically, from the site of my own failure, and I begin preparing for the challenge ahead. I drink no alcohol. I eat no sugar. In addition to doing soccer drills and scrimmages, I work out twice daily at a training facility in the Home Depot Center. I watch my body wake up and change, the ridges of muscles rising up, the ropy veins twitching along the length of my limbs. With every hoist of the weights and lap around the track I remind myself what's at stake: after these games, the 99ers are retiring. I ruined their final World Cup, and now I have a chance—no, a responsibility—to make it up to them and to redeem myself in the process. By early August, when we leave for training camp in Crete, I'll be a different person, as different as if I'd reconfigured the cells inside my blood.

My resolve remains even as my love life becomes unexpectedly complicated. Since starting training, I've noticed a woman who's working as a nanny for our assistant coach. Her name is Haley, and she's my usual type: confident, athletic, feminine. I have no idea if she's into girls until one day, when I step off the bus, she lays a hand on my shoulder, her fingers curling against my bare skin. There is something so strangely intimate about the touch, the delicate but purposeful dig of her nails, that I stop, my foot raised in midair. *What the hell was that?* I think, and try to dismiss it. I'm still dating Nikki, and she's scheduled to fly in from New York for a visit, and the last thing I need right now is to muddle through a long-distance breakup.

The following week, during Nikki's visit, we're out to dinner when my phone rings: Haley.

"Let's go get a drink and take a walk," she says.

"Wait, *what?*" is my smooth reply.

I can hear her inhale, a sharp intake of breath.

"How about a drink and a walk?" she tries again, this time as a question.

There is nothing I want more, I decide, and realize I have two options: break up with Nikki as soon as possible, abbreviating our visit; or string her along for the week only to surprise her when she gets home. I go with number one, and Nikki flies out the following morning. But of course I still feel like a jerk when I pick up the phone and call Haley.

We meet for dinner at a sushi place on the ocean. I remember her shirt, green-and-white striped, and the flush of her cheeks from the sun. She has sake, and I briefly repress Intense Abby and order a glass of wine. Afterward we stroll to the pier. It's closed, so we take turns hurdling the fence, and we have miles of beach to ourselves, the ocean lapping at our calves.

She kisses me and digs her nails into my shoulder in that same way, and I fall in love instantly; a part of me is in love with her still.

We see each other as often as possible during training. Every time I travel with the team I head to her apartment as soon as I return. She gives me a set of keys, and once she comes home to find me lying in the middle of her floor, naked, with our favorite soundtrack playing. I buy her five-thousand-dollar earrings. We laugh and talk for hours. I want to know everything: where she's been, where she's going, what she's been through, what she's conquered, what she's lost. She coins a phrase for how she feels after our marathon dates: the "Abby Hangover." She jostles every other thought out of my mind until it's time to leave for Greece. Only then do I invoke the memory of the Germans celebrating the World Cup, and I bring that anger with me.

We're up 1–0 against Brazil in the Olympic final, but the game is not going well. The Brazilians play with skill and flamboyance, as though we're at a dance party rather than the Olympics, as though this is fun and not war. We're slow and disorganized, failing to find each other, and the only reason we survive is because Brazil clinks the ball, twice, off the goalposts. With seventeen minutes left in regulation, our luck runs out: a Brazilian player named Pretinha, my former teammate on the Washington Freedom, shoots a line drive into the net, tying the game.

The pressure fuels me, catering to my need for extremes; I do not know how to exist in the middle. I unleash my old failures and let them run free inside of me, filling me up with a wild rage. I am a cocked gun, a sharpened knife, a grenade with its pin half pulled. In the 112th minute, I see my chance in the form of a corner kick, and I leap, unfurling my long body, snapping my head—contact, and the sweet, fleeting blackout before I realize what I've done.

In the locker room, amid sprays of champagne, Julie Foudy turns to me. "Thank you," she says, "for not making the next forty years of my life miserable." Mia is next, and speaks of leaving the program in the hands of the next generation. For the first time I realize that my life is about to change, radically and irrevocably. It's the beginning of my turn.

In the fall, after a nine-game victory tour with the national team, I plan something I've never done before: a solo trip, two weeks of hiking and camping in the Arizona desert. For the first time in a long time I am at peace, both with my accomplishments and with who I am, and I want to preserve the feeling, tuck it away for safekeeping. Even in my euphoric state, I know the day will come when I'll need to summon it as a reminder.

While I was away, a friend borrowed my Jeep and drove it down to Florida, so first I need to fly south to pick it up. I stop by Are's parents' house to show them my gold medal, which I couldn't bear to leave at home. More than an athletic honor, I view it as a time divider for my life, Before Gold and After Gold, a reminder of where I've been and where I need to go. I have an itinerary, but I expect that I'll improvise, Intense Abby and Chill Abby in perfect accord.

I start heading west, intending to stop first in Flagstaff. An hour into the drive, I feel an odd flicker of unease, a sudden and persistent sense that something's gone wrong. Panicked, I stop at a gas station, load up on cigarettes, tobacco, coffee, and energy drinks, and drive thirty-two hours straight, taking a slight detour to Haley's house in Phoenix, where she now attends school. I can't help but break our newly enacted pact: we'd decided to take some time apart and meet next year in the Grand Canyon if we missed each other.

By the time I arrive it's sunrise, and I press her buzzer, holding my finger down until she appears at the door. I am wild-eyed and delirious and soaked in crazy, but I don't care; I need to see her expression in order to know the truth. I ask her to tell it to me, straight and honest, as we've always been.

Taking my hand, she leads me to the driveway, where we sit on the trunk of her car. She tilts her face toward mine and confesses that she's slept with someone else.

"Who?" I ask, my voice sounding small and far away.

"You don't know him," she says.

Him.

I'm too wired to cry, and instead I resume the smoking, chewing, and chugging as I drive the final two hours to Flagstaff. Lying sleepless under the stars, I try to convince myself it's okay to be alone.

Next on my list is Sedona, famous for its vortex sites, mysterious pockets of amplified energy, allegedly capable of healing both physical and psychological pain. I plan to stay there for only two days—I still want to see Moab and Bryce Canyon—but find myself unable to move on, drawn by the mystique of its powers, even though I don't entirely believe in them.

I stop in a diner and realize it's Thanksgiving, the first I've ever spent alone, and I imagine my parents and siblings and their combined children sitting around the table, loud enough to be heard down the street. I slide into a booth, scanning the menu, and can't help but eavesdrop on the family sitting behind me—mother, father, and young girl, their plates piled high with turkey and stuffing. I turn my head just enough to gauge the kid's age, surmising she's about seven or eight.

"You really need to find a good man," the mother says, and I sit straighter in my booth. "You need to find a good man to have a good life, just like I found your father."

The words stir a fury inside of me. I think about where I am: twenty-four years old, just a few steps away from being a powerful, self-sufficient woman, someone who never considered relying on a man or anyone else for my well-being and success, someone with an Olympic gold medal hidden just yards away from this spot.

I twist in my seat, poking my head into their space. I open my mouth and am prepared to voice a tumble of thoughts: *Lady, just shut the fuck up. SHUT UP. Don't diminish your daughter! What you're doing right now is giving her an out to rely on someone else, and in this world, if you rely on other people, they take advantage of you. In this world, if you rely on other people, you don't get to where you want to go. You get to a version of yourself, a small portion of yourself, and never learn how to access the whole thing.*

Instead of delivering this monologue, I tap the little girl on the shoulder and ask if I might borrow her coloring book.

To this day I think about that little girl and about myself in that pivotal time back in 2004, when I was old enough to have tasted success, but young enough not to fear its consequences. I still wish I'd said something to counteract her mother's words—and, while I was at it, warned my future self that I wouldn't have all the answers, and that having answers still doesn't prevent life from taking unexpected turns.

8

DEPRESSIVE

There are cycles to soccer that, I'm learning, correspond to cycles within myself. Several years of quiet work leads to a few short weeks on the international stage where, win or lose, we descend back down the mountain and prepare to climb all over again. After the high of the Olympics, followed by the news of Haley's betrayal, I crave that period of hibernation, the chance to feed myself in ways that have nothing to do with the sport. It's an escalation of the pattern I began in high school, when I first realized that soccer is bearable only if I take time to rebel against it.

When I get back to my old apartment in Washington, D.C., I call Are.

"Where should I move?" I ask him. "Los Angeles or San Francisco?"

"L.A.," he says without hesitation.

After scouring the Internet for a condo, I buy one in Hermosa Beach, sight unseen, with my post-Olympic money, and tell Are he's coming to live with me.

We move in June 2005 and settle into an unconventional domestic routine, grilling out every night and joining a touch football league, playing on the beach. "As far as I'm concerned," Are muses, "every woman is a lesbian unless she says otherwise." Occasionally, and only half in jest, he brushes a hand across my breast, testing to see how quickly I slap it away. I reconnect with Haley, talking frequently on the phone and traveling to Phoenix for occasional visits. I develop a taste for red wine that rivals my love of vodka cocktails and Labatt's beer; Are and I often finish three bottles over the course of a meal.

I meet a new friend, Kara, who works as the team's sports therapist. We're both Geminis, born four days apart, and she understands my dual—and occasionally dueling—personalities better than anyone. Right away I can tell she speaks her mind, even if the thought is one I'd rather not hear, a quality I'll come to depend upon in the months and years ahead.

The dynamics on the team are changing as swiftly and dramatically as I am. We have a new coach, Greg Ryan, and only four of the 99ers remain: Kristine Lilly, Kate Markgraf, goalkeeper Briana Scurry, and Christie Rampone—still known as

"Pearcie" to us, after her maiden name, and briefly on leave to have her first child. Our new roster includes a dozen players who are twenty-three or younger and a dozen who have played in five or fewer games. At twenty-five, with sixty caps under my belt, I am a grizzled veteran, and I begin to act like it, ordering people to hustle at practice and critiquing their play, being every bit as blunt as I am when I critique myself. The 2007 World Cup is still more than a year away, but I am already fearful of repeating the failures of the last one.

We start another residency camp at the Home Depot Center, three weeks on and one week off. After practice one afternoon, a teammate casually mentions Haley's engagement. I freeze, locker door half open. *Engagement*. I can't imagine why she would do such a thing without telling me, or even how she could do such a thing in the first place. Clearly she's willing to risk losing me for good. My mind treads back to its well-worn truisms: I am unloved. I am unlovable. I am abandoned and forgotten. Even if I force myself to be seen, I will never truly be found.

As soon as I get home, I sit on the edge of my bed and summon the will to call her, afraid of what I might hear. After three rings she picks up.

"Hal," I say, my voice cracking on that one syllable.

"Hey!" she says cheerfully, and I suspect she knows what's coming.

"I heard something really weird, and I don't know how to say this—it's so bizarre." I laugh meekly, as if the very thought of it is too absurd to consider. "Are you . . . *engaged*?"

She's quiet a moment, and admits, "Oh yeah, I am."

I probe, needing to know every last torturous detail. Her fiancé isn't the man she slept with when we were dating, the man she told me about before I drove off into the desert. This is a different man, a man she'd never once mentioned in all our long conversations, hours I spent hoping we might try again. *This* man surprised her with a trip to Mount McKinley, hiking with her to the summit, where she turned to find him on bended knee. She keeps talking, and every word is an internal earthquake, each more powerful than the last, carving a fault line from my throat to my heart and splitting me in half. "I still love you," I hear her say, "and that won't change."

"What the fuck?" I say, screaming now. "How can you be getting married to this man when you have feelings for another person?"

"I'm different than you. I'm not going to lie to you and tell you I don't love you."

"Wouldn't you think I needed to hear that *before* you decided to marry him?" I'm sobbing now, and mortified that I've allowed such emotion to escape.

She's quiet, out of things to say.

"I don't know how to process this," I whisper, and hang up.

I lied, unwittingly. I do know how to process it, or at least attempt to process it—by numbing it out of existence. I develop my own interpretation of Newton's third law: calculated actions to further my career collide with an equally strong desire to destroy myself. For the three weeks I'm at camp I'm all business, running drills and practicing headers and solidifying my role as leader, and during my off week I drink until I can't talk or stand or even see. This isn't Chill Abby, searching for fun and levity amidst a successful career, but a warped, corrupted version of Intense Abby, with all her focus and ambition turned inward and darkened.

Are, my perennial drinking buddy, never chastises me or even advises me to take a night off, but Kara, my sports therapist (and voice of reason), does. One night we're all out at a gay bar in West Hollywood, and some strange girl pushes my friend. I put down my vodka and step forward. "Don't push her," I say, enunciating each word. I think the matter is settled until we go to leave, and suddenly I'm wearing someone on my back, and there are four or five women pummeling any part of me they can reach. I swing wildly, hearing the smack of flesh and feeling my knuckles sting, until I'm on my knees, crying, and Are scoops me up.

"Where are you responsible, Abby?" Kara asks. "Put yourself in places where you can answer that question. You can be so sweet and loving and kind, and then there's this other person, who's so wounded and upset and on a rampage." Sometimes when we're out and I'm too drunk to know my own name, she calls me "Mary," afraid that someone might recognize me.

I am Mary one night at a bar where the bouncer refuses to let us in, explaining they're at capacity. Gathering all of my seventy-one inches, spreading my body as tall and wide as it will go, I thrust my face into his, eye to eye, nose to nose.

"Do you know who I am?" I say, a question that now makes me cringe.

"Come on, *Mary,*" Kara says, pulling on my arm.

"I don't give a fuck who you are," he responds, so close I can't see his pupils, so close our lips nearly touch.

Pathetically, I'm about to try again—*Motherfucker, do you know who I am?*—when Kara manages to peel me away, and I flip the question inward, interrogating myself. *No, motherfucker, I don't know who you are, and at this rate I probably never will.*

9

CAPTAIN

The cycle of soccer spins inexorably forward, taking me along with it, and as the World Cup approaches I emerge from hibernation, shedding my vices and sharpening my focus. But for the first time in my career my body is not co-operating, opening itself up to injuries it has always managed to avoid. In early November 2006, during a tournament in South Korea, I roll my ankle so badly I think it's broken. Just a sprain, the trainers determine, and after they shoot me up with cortisone and swaddle it in a thick wad of tape, I'm good to go again. A few weeks later, the cortisone flowing and the tape still intact, I score both goals in a 2–0 game against Mexico, qualifying us for the 2007 World Cup.

I think the worst is over, but the ankle injury has a domino effect, spilling into the rest of my body. Before we leave for Shanghai, during a warm-up game against Finland, my big toe collides with another player's leg. I can feel the toe swelling inside my cleat, throbbing against the leather, but I keep playing until the twenty-seventh minute, when it can no longer withstand an ounce of pressure. During the first game of the World Cup, with toe numbed and ankle wrapped, my head rams against the head of a North Korean player, as solidly as a bowling ball striking a pin. The back of my head splits open. Blood seeps from my scalp and trickles to my neck, and in this condition I walk 150 yards to the locker room at the end of the stadium for stitches. During the ten minutes I'm out, our 1–0 lead becomes a 2–1 deficit, and we finish at a 2–2 tie. I begin a revolving cocktail of pills: Vicodin, caffeine, and Ambien.

Before the semifinals, where we'll face Brazil—ostentatious, dramatic Brazil—Coach Ryan makes a controversial decision, benching our goalkeeper, Hope Solo, in favor of Briana Scurry, a 99er who's set to retire soon. From start to finish the game is a disaster. Our set pieces falter and fail. Our defense is tentative and porous. We lose a key player, midfielder Shannon Boxx, late in the first half after she receives a red card. In the end we're routed 4–0 and left in shock as the Brazilians mob each other on the field.

On the bus ride back to the hotel, everything hurts: my ankle, my toe, my head, my heart, my pride. This was not only my chance at redemption for the last disappointing World Cup, it was also my first major test as a leader of this team. Once again I've let everyone down, myself included, and I feel dressed head to toe in failure, wearing my shame like a second skin. I ache to dull both my throbbing joints and my roiling thoughts, so I pop a few Ambien, and then a few more, wishing I had some vodka to wash them down.

I'm back in my room, prone on my bed, when one of my teammates bursts in. "Did you see the fucking thing Hope said?" she asks. I haven't, but it's all over the news. In an interview after the match, Hope claimed, "There's no doubt in my mind I would have made those saves."

There's an unspoken code in our sport, with a few key tenets: you don't talk shit about your teammates, you don't throw anyone under the bus, and you don't publicly promote yourself at the expense of the team. The comment further derails a team that had veered off track, and when the tournament is finally over I make a promise to myself: if I'm ever forced to ride the bench, for any reason, I will not react in a manner I'll later regret.

Once I'm home in Hermosa Beach, down from the mountain and settling into the valley, depression creeps back into my psyche. "I'm the saddest person I have ever known," I text to Are's mom, Dena. I fight to reconcile this feeling with my public and professional persona: fun, optimistic, inspiring, driven. It's a stubborn, intrepid gloom, stalking me with the skill and fervor of a private eye, finding me no matter how much I hide inside the numbness of booze and pills. My body activates its freakish internal scale, measuring the maximum amount of alcohol it can handle without affecting my game.

It sustains the balance perfectly during our post–World Cup "celebration" tour in October, when we play three games against Mexico in three different cities. I start dating a new teammate, but as much as I like her, I'm still fixated on Haley and still wallowing in the old wounds stirred up by her betrayal.

A few weeks before Christmas, the team convenes in Los Angeles for a four-day camp. After the World Cup, Greg Ryan was fired, and we have a new coach, Pia Sundhage, a veteran Swedish soccer player so revered in her home country that her image once graced a postage stamp. We also have new young players and a new captain, Pearcie, ready to play only 112 days after giving birth. Pearcie and I have a tacit agreement: she's the arm-banded captain, the official face of the team, the wise and calm general who dispenses strategy before battle begins. I'm her obnoxious counterpart, the trusty lieutenant who incentivizes her teammates to kill.

A few of the veteran leaders, myself included, meet privately with Pia to discuss what happened at the World Cup. This team has a chemistry problem, we argue, and it's going to be a problem moving forward if we want to win games. Pia's answer is concise and leaves no room for debate: "Hope is the goalkeeper. You guys have to figure this out and deal with it."

When the rest of the team joins us, she pulls out a guitar and sings Bob Dylan in faltering English: "For the times they are a-changin'." It's an obvious plea to move past the World Cup debacle, but I apply the words personally. The 2008 Olympics are fast approaching, and it's about time to emerge from my darkness, to peer out from the cave and find my other self.

Before I leave, Pia asks to speak to me alone.

"Listen," she says, "I don't want you to have to worry about being a captain and dealing with that stuff. I want you to just worry about scoring goals."

"I'm fine with that," I assure her. "I want to worry about scoring goals, but I'm also still going to lead. So you're going to get, like, three birds with two stones."

I leave camp feeling happier than I have in a year. Some disagreements and resentments linger, but the World Cup drama now seems muted and surmountable. Collectively, we're the best in the world, and we all need each other to win.

Once again I remove all vices from my life, instantly and easily, as if they're accessories one season out of style. My freakish internal scale recalibrates its settings so that even an ounce of contraband is rejected. Booze, sugar, fried food, junk television—anything that sullies my body or mind—cease to exist for this finite stretch of time. On the advice of my doctors, I still allow pills into my regimen: caffeine, Vicodin, and Ambien, in carefully regulated turns, all of them now necessary for Intense Abby to perform as expected, by herself and the world.

By July 16, five days before we leave for Beijing, I am a sleek and lucid beast, ready to steamroll my path to the goal. Injuries aside, I have never felt so fit and focused and certain of victory. On this night we have an exhibition against Brazil in San Diego, our last game before the Olympics begins, and the team finally feels cohesive, ready to play for another gold.

In the locker room, Pearcie motions everyone to gather for our pregame talk. Her advice is practical and precise, spoken in the language all of us know best: "We want to go out and really defend, and we want to switch the point of attack. Then, of course, we want to get numbers in the box and score goals."

Out on the field we bend into our huddle, faces close and arms intertwined behind backs. It's my turn to speak.

"We have to go out and play for each other," I say. "If we're all on the same page we can do that. Every time you put this jersey on it means something." My voice amplifies. "We got this! We *got* this! We fuck . . . fucking . . ." and my words trip over each other, tumbling out in the wrong order and making no sense at all. "My god," I finish, "I'm such an idiot," and everyone laughs. I understand, then, that we all needed to laugh; it's the only thing that cuts the pregame tension. "Whatever," I add, slapping my forehead. "Pearcie!"

On cue, Pearcie thrusts her hand in the middle of the circle, waiting for our hands to stack on top. "Oosa on three!" she calls, our phonetic abbreviation for "USA." And we respond in fevered unison: "Oosa, Oosa, Oosa, Ah!"

The night air is hot, so hot I imagine steam hissing up from the field, marking the spots where my cleats have stepped. We're hustling, pressing the Brazilians, stifling their freewheeling style. At all times I'm attuned to where the ball is, like a pointer dog identifying its prey, and I am running as fast as I ever have, gaining speed. Cheers from the crowd rise up to follow me, and as I'm about to make my move I am stopped by the point of my opponent's knee. It stabs at my leg with superhuman ferocity. I feel my left leg leave itself. I'm on the ground, now, with a clear view, and see that my foot and my thigh are turned in opposite directions, as if in a disagreement that can never be resolved.

My mind, hyperattuned, delivers its diagnosis: both the tibia and fibula are broken. Another realization crests to the surface: the team leaves for the Olympics in five days, and I am not going to be on that plane. Inside my vortex of thoughts, depression buds and takes root. *Not now,* I think, and swat it away. Later I'll have plenty of time to tend to it and feed it and watch it grow, but now I have to be on my game. I have to be a captain.

Without question it is the worst physical pain I've ever endured. Worse than my ankle, worse than my toe, worse than the gash in my scalp. It's worse, too, than pain that is yet to come: Achilles tendinitis, a sprained knee, a torn quad, a broken nose, and blackened eyes. A collision that splits my hairline like a coconut, requiring staples to hold it together long enough for me to finish the game. A concussion after which I am not in my sane mind, playing without the ability to see the ball at all.

Lying on the field, I think of my parents, watching back home in Rochester, eagerly awaiting their trip to China for the Olympics. Over the years we've devised a system: if I'm ever down, I give a thumbs-up so that they know I'm okay. This time I leave my thumb down, and instead beckon the trainers to come straightaway.

Pearcie gets there first.

"What happened?" she asks, squatting down. Her proximity is a small comfort.

"I broke my leg. My tib and fib are both broken."

"Are you sure?"

"Yeah," I concede, and my mind veers right back to the game. "Tell Pia to get a sub ready."

The emergency crew rolls a stretcher toward me. I feel my left leg being encased and my body lifting off the ground. It's dark as the ambulance doors close by my feet. My leg feels like it's harboring a detonated bomb. Someone stabs a needle into my arm, and the pain begins to subside tentatively, by increments.

"Can I borrow a phone?" I ask no one in particular, and a medic obliges. I dial Lauren Cheney, a new teammate who also plays forward. She hadn't made the Olympic roster a few weeks ago, but I think she's up to the job.

"Cheney," I say, without greeting or preamble. "I hope you've been working out. I'm injured, and if they replace me with another forward it's going to be you."

She laughs. "Shut up, you're being dramatic. You're fine, you're always fine."

"I'm serious," I reiterate. "I can't run. So *you* need to get fit, because you're going to the Olympics."

I hang up and call my parents. They were watching the game on television, and my mother already has plane reservations for the next flight out. The pain medicine creeps further into my bloodstream. "I want my mom," I whisper, hanging up, and the dial tone lures me into a restless sleep.

10

LEADER

It takes the doctors four hours to piece me back together again. They create a complex patchwork of screws and insert a titanium rod through my knee, piercing the bone marrow of the tibia, connecting the two broken halves. A few teammates are waiting in my hospital room when they wheel me in after surgery, high as a loon. My eyes make out blurred features and distorted voices: Pearcie, Kate Markgraf, Angela Hucles, Heather O'Reilly, Leslie Osborne. Others come and go as I drift in and out. Someone brings me my phone and computer. I'm coherent enough to search my name and "broken leg" and watch the resulting video clips, each showing my agony from a different angle.

"Can you please stop watching that?" someone asks.

She—I'm not quite sure who it is—means well, but no, I can't stop; my brain demands evidence that I'm not caught in some prolonged and intractable nightmare. I try to respond. My tongue is heavy inside my mouth and the words have to sluice around it, like river water around a rock. "I just can't believe this happened," I hear myself say. "It's so weird. I don't get hurt. I can play through anything." Silently I continue the conversation: *I did everything right this time; I was prepared and centered and controlled.* And then comes the silent response: *When are you going to learn you can't control everything?*

My mother arrives, and I weep again at the sight of her. I ask for my watch, which she fastens around my wrist. Every eight minutes I'm allowed to press the button for another shot of morphine; I set my timer so as not to fall behind. When my phone rings, my mother hands it to me. It's my girlfriend and my mother leaves the room to let me talk.

She asks how I am, tells me she's so sorry. After a few moments of commiserating, she gets to the point. "I can't do this," she confesses, as kindly as she can. She elaborates: We keep getting injured. It's a sign we're not meant to be together. We need a break. She hopes I understand . . .

I'm crying again when my mother returns, and I calm down just enough to relate the gist of the conversation. She sits on the edge of the bed, stroking my hair. "She doesn't deserve your tears," she says, proving that she, at least, has accepted what she can't control. She's had a few lessons in that regard; my sister Laura has also come out as a lesbian.

I doze and tap my morphine button, again and again, a slurry, slow-motion dance: *doze and tap, doze and tap*. In the midst of one interval, I ask my mother for my computer. Opening my e-mail, I find a message from Haley, and am suddenly and strangely alert:

> Abby, that did not look good. What happened to you just now? Holy fuck. I just saw you say it was broken. You are a horse, a workhorse, and I hope so much that this injury is not as bad as it seems.
>
> Your team and coaching staff looked blanched on TV. I could see the color leave their faces simultaneously. You have their respect and admiration; that is so evident. Their leader was leaving. I could see how much you bring to that team, and the respect those you lead have for you. You were brave, too, twenty times more calm than I was on the couch. You have so much support and love. I am so sorry for this. I am sick to my stomach and upset and I can imagine you're in shock. I am so sorry.
>
> Love,
>
> Haley

Immediately I open a new message and begin typing:

> Hey, at the moment it's 4:10 A.M. on Friday. I can't sleep so I grabbed my computer and saw your e-mail. Thanks for your words. They meant a lot. It was so weird because right

when it happened I knew. I felt the bones snap. I saw exactly what you saw on television. So whenever everyone else was freaking out, I couldn't.

Hilarious that I was trying to lessen the blow for other people. Because honestly, it is okay. I am okay. My leg hurts like hell and this situation sucks pretty bad, but there are way worse things in life. And maybe I'm just in denial or something, but immediately I went to the positives and just focused on those. I am bummed for my teammates as I am kind of important for this team, so it's tough bearing this sort of responsibility for them but it would be cool for them to overcome this and win it anyway. It would just be amazing to me.

I can't believe you still watch my games. I don't say that because I want you to affirm anything to me, just that I am surprised that you do. A few questions for you: How are you/what are you doing these days? I am going to have a lot more time on my hands these next few months. Any good ideas for me? Remember, I'll be on crutches, so hiking and stuff will be out of the question.

I had a feeling a few weeks back that you're preggo. Could this be true? Or am I just nuts? Thanks for the e-mail, Hal. It meant a lot. If you want, call. It would be nice to catch up. I felt the love you sent. Much appreciated. Sending mine back . . .

They release me, sending me back to my Hermosa Beach condo, where Kara is waiting to take care of me. She replaced Are as my roommate after he moved back to Florida to start a personal training business. I'm grateful; I need her calm, sensible perspective right now. I return to the hospital for rehab and am eager to start, if only to regain a sense of control.

At first we try three hours per day, rotating my ankle and contracting my quad to fire up the muscle, which seems to have atrophied overnight. I limp up and down the hallways, a trainer on either side. I develop a tolerance for Vicodin, demand more, and am furious when I'm denied. The team doctor has to talk me down, explaining that the synapses in my brain are firing differently; there's going to be trial and error in finding the right cocktail, a healthy balance of numbing and riding out the pain. He was there when it happened—in fact, he *heard* it happen, all the way from his seat in the stadium. I need to accept the fact that this is going to hurt, and that it's going to take time, more time than I probably imagine, more time than I've ever had to give anything else.

After the day's rehab, with nothing but time, I attempt to be a leader from sixty-two hundred miles away. I contemplate flying to China to surprise my team, but during an acupuncture appointment, with needles protruding like quills from head to toe, I conclude that my presence would only be a distraction. Instead, I decide to write them a letter, some words to inspire them before the games begin.

I open a new e-mail and begin: "To the U.S. Olympic Women's National Soccer Team" (God, what a *loser,* I think years later, in my postretirement hotel room). And from there

I write as if possessed, the words lining up in my mind and my fingers unable to stop.

I am hoping to somehow inspire you guys, and I thought my being there could do just that. But the truth is, I'm not the inspiration. It's the situation that's inspiring—and you do not in fact need me there.

I thought a lot about my injury, and what keeps coming up for me is that this has happened for a reason. It makes me realize that this team has to find its way without me. What's so amazing about this whole thing is that every one of you has the opportunity to truly become the best of champions. This is so fitting in terms of the way things have gone all year. I have done everything and then some that has been asked of me; you all have done everything and then some that has been asked of you. You have turned over every stone, and Pia is all about challenges. So why not embrace this one? Because the truth is that this challenge that's in front of you will in fact define this team. Not to stress you all out, but it gives me chilly bumps just thinking about it.

It's a simple question: How do you want this team to be remembered? And I know you're probably all really sick of getting questions about how things will turn out without me on the field. I'm sorry about that. I'm sure it's annoying, but really, it's a great question and I hope you all have talked about it or at least sat with it because it's going to be what everyone wants to see.

I can safely say that I have no doubt you all will rise to the occasion. No doubt at all, because that's what this team is, has been, and will always be. It's timeless and no one person decides its fate. Do you all feel that? Do you all understand that? I feel like that was the lesson I really learned last year during the World Cup. Obviously I didn't fully grasp it. I do now. I have been totally humbled by this whole thing and hope that you all have been too. Things have changed, and you all need to believe that you can do this.

Look around the room. Look each other in the eyes. This is a team that will win gold, and you can't doubt that for one second. Yeah, you're going to make mistakes. Yes, you will be nervous. Yes, goals may get scored. It's not about what happens; it's about how you react to all of it. If you let doubt seep in for just a moment then you won't succeed. I promise you that. So if you make a bad pass or you miss an open girl or you can't find anything good about your game, just look around. Look where you are. See that you're playing not to win, but to define yourself.

You are playing to make your mark on this game. It's honor that you're in search of, and if you stop thinking so hard about success or failure and instead focus on each other, you will find way more than honor. You will find the purest part of what makes all of this so special.

I have felt that once before—four years ago, at our last Olympics. Some of you haven't ever felt it. Some have felt it more than me. But this will be different from anything else you've ever experienced before. I just know it. Can you? Do you feel what an opportunity this is? Are you in control of how it plays out? You all have a choice. Are you going to cry into a corner or will you stand up and fight? What are you willing to give? Because it takes more than what you think you're even capable of. But that's what these kinds of tournaments are about. The team that's standing on top of the tallest podium will have gone past their own limitations. They will have believed in each other 100 percent of the time. They will have enjoyed the process. They will have overcome problems, and most importantly the team that is standing on the podium getting the gold medal wrapped around their necks will have done it together.

I believe in my heart that every one of you can and will make that commitment to one another, that no matter what you will do whatever it takes to experience that moment together. It will be supreme and I would love nothing more than to see that happen. I hope you all feel that you are ready for that.

By the time I type that last period, I'm sweating and slightly out of breath. I'm not finished, and my fingers start tapping again; I want to address each teammate personally, one by one.

I tell Nicole Barnhart that while we all might mercilessly mock her compression socks, she's clearly the toughest chick on the team.

I tell Heather Mitts what I've been thinking since our days in college—that she has the best legs I've ever seen and that she is the most consistent player. Plus, she never lets me beat her during drills, and fuck, does that piss me off.

I tell Pearcie what she already knows: She's been my rock the past few years. She's solid, loyal, kind, strong, stubborn, and keeps secrets better than anyone I know.

I marvel at Rachel Buehler's fearlessness. I laud Lindsay Tarpley for her impeccable work ethic. I tell Natasha Kai that her passion is inspiring. I admire Shannon Boxx's willingness to attack every opportunity. I thank Amy Rodriguez for enduring my lengthy ruminations when we roomed together last year in China. I praise Heather O'Reilly's huge heart and six-pack abs. I get metaphysical on Aly Wagner and tell her, "Your being is special." I call Carli Lloyd the most gifted player I've ever known, and admonish anyone who dismisses her just because she's from New Jersey.

I note that Tobin Heath is wise beyond her years, and the most "going-the-full" person in history. I acknowledge Stephanie Cox's willingness to have uncomfortable conversations. I call Kate Markgraf the most underrated player in the history of this national team. I appreciate that Angela Hucles has a perspective on life that is so perfectly and uniquely her own. I tell Lori Chalupny—"Chupes"—that she always brings two words to mind: *most solid*. I am blown away by Briana Scurry's strength, and I ask her to share her valuable secrets with all of us.

I thank Lauren Cheney for stepping in to replace me, and tell her it's her time now—her turn. I apologize to Hope Solo, admitting that our World Cup disaster forced me to do some soul-searching. Instead of being honest and compassionate, I was controlling and manipulative. And in moving forward, I promise to get past my own ego and learn to trust. I tell her not to be afraid to show the world her softer side. I know it's there, I say, because I've seen it.

By now I'm crying again, and aching for Vicodin, and the laptop lies hot across my thighs. My stiff fingers push to conclude:

"So that's it," I write. "I'm sorry this has been so long, but it's important for me to express my thoughts clearly, and I know I even failed at that. I guess I've said it all. I love you all so fucking much and I'm so sorry I'm not there with you physically. I am with you, though. If you make a mistake or you're scared or you don't know what to do, just know that I am with you. Just feel me by your side. I am there. Open your hearts and you'll know. If you do, you will be champions. But it has to be a commitment from everyone. You can do this. You can win. I just know it. Good luck and play your hearts out. I'll be watching."

I'm watching from my couch when we play Norway on August 6. We look lost out there, timid and defanged, and I scream at the TV through my Vicodin haze: *No, Jesus, no—what are you doing? Get on your mark! Move, move! Fuck, fuck!* My tirade awakens my neighbor all the way from across the street. It's nearly dawn when he rings my doorbell, and Kara jumps up to answer.

"Can you please quiet down?" he asks.

"Sorry!" I call from the couch. "We'll try to be more quiet."

As he leaves, he lets his dog take a piss on our doorstep.

Fuck it, I think. *I'm going to be loud as I want.* My boisterous armchair coaching has no effect, and we lose 2–0.

I pop a few Ambien and sleep off my sorrow.

We have better luck in the next few rounds, beating Japan, New Zealand, and Canada. In the semifinals we face Japan again, and for this game I fly out to New York, crutching my way through the airport and wincing at the turbulence. When I land, Are is there to greet me; he flew up from Florida so we could watch the game together. We drive upstate to the Thousand Islands, a cluster of islands that straddles the U.S.–Canadian border, where my parents own a plot of land and a secluded, ancient house.

Their island has always been my favorite place, my sanctuary where I can rewind time and forget, where nothing and no one can find me. The house itself still has old half-doors, designed so that the original owner could hunt ducks from the comfort of his living room, and an intricate tin ceiling that catches and throws the light. There's no electricity, just a generator; as kids we had no choice but to talk to each other, an extension of our strict dinnertime rules from home.

Usually I appreciate the quiet time, the forced lack of access to television, but right now my team is about to play Japan and I could really use one. An idea sparks: We take a boat ride across the bay to a new house, a sort of rustic

McMansion, and ask the owners if they'd be so kind as to let us watch the game there. We settle in on their couch, only to realize that this house is on the Canadian side of the Saint Lawrence River, and the local station is not broadcasting the American game. Are and I exchange panicked glances—*shit, what are we going to do?*—and we decide we'll figure it out on the boat ride back to our side of the water.

We dock our boat at the edge of a town called Alexandria Bay, and I hobble as quickly as I can, while Are looks out for stones that might trip me. We spot a convenience store with a TV affixed to the ceiling. From the running ticker on the bottom of the screen I can see we're losing, 1–0, but the store doesn't subscribe to the universal sports channel. It's about six in the morning, too early for any bars to be open, and I am running out of options, crutch-pacing back and forth, worried about plays I can't see. Desperate, I approach the woman at the counter.

"Do you know anyone who has DirecTV?" I ask.

"My son does," she says, "but he lives a bit out of town."

I'm frantic enough to risk imposing on her. "Could you please take us there?" I ask, and explain who I am and why I'm not in Beijing.

She takes pity on me and agrees, and I text my parents and siblings, telling them to come along.

We all pile into her van. She introduces herself as the "the Mayor of Alexandria Bay," but please, call her "the Mayor" for short. Her home is hidden away on the far side of a trailer park, and her son lives in the adjacent detached garage, a setup that reminds me of sneaking around with Teddy, my high school boyfriend. Most of the town is still sleeping, including the Mayor's son, and she has to knock on his door repeatedly to wake him up.

He appears, rubbing sleep from his eyes. "What's going on?"

"She's on the girls' national soccer team," the Mayor explains, pointing at me, "and she's injured. Her team is playing and she needs your TV."

This stranger invites my entire family in and, for the next hour, allows us to commandeer his house. So far Japan has scored the only goal of the game, and the play is a frenzied reel of agonizing near-misses: Heather O'Reilly's cross-shot is repelled by a diving save; Amy Rodriguez shoots into the box but fails to find a teammate; a Japanese defender finagles the ball from Angela Hucles, flattening our momentum. Now Japan is in control, the ball bouncing from player to player, two dozen touches in a row. I brace myself, waiting for them to score again, and then . . . *holy shit*: Heather sprints past her defender and blasts a firecracker to Angela, alone near the box. She guides it in, and we're tied. Three minutes later, Lori Chalupny performs a magical ballet across the field, swiveling past and through defenders, launching a shot just seconds before being cornered by another. She makes it, and we're ahead, 2–1. After halftime, in the seventieth minute, Heather lobs a shot, merely hoping to get the ball in the box, but it soars in just below the bar—goal! A few plays later, Angela kicks the ball from a ridiculously sharp angle—another seemingly accidental goal. Thankfully, those count, too, and now it's 4–1. Japan manages to score once more, in the third and final minute of extra time, but we hang on to the lead. I thank our host for his hospitality, and we make the trip home to the other side of the river.

For the gold medal game against Brazil, I'm more prepared, having confirmed with a local diner that they would be airing the game. As soon as they open we all slide into booths, with me on the end so I can stretch my leg and shake my crutch at the screen. I'm too nervous to eat breakfast, and my omelet congeals on its plate as I watch Marta, Brazil's formidable and flashy leader, twist and spin her way across the field, looking more like a samba dancer than a forward—"Pelé with skirts," they call her, a moniker reportedly bestowed by Pelé himself. In the eighteenth minute Pearcie closes her down, but Marta again finds her rhythm, veering around our defenders, cocking her foot, and propelling it square into the ball—a beautiful shot, I have to admit. My breath halts in the back of my throat. . . . It's wide! A miss! I exhale.

The Brazilians excel at the art of drawing fouls; one mild collision and their players fling themselves to the ground, flailing and barrel-rolling as if trying to escape flames. A Brazilian named Formiga tries this trick after colliding with Heather Mitts in the thirty-seventh minute, but thankfully the referee isn't impressed. At halftime both sides are still scoreless, and the diner is filling up with patrons, some of whom recognize me (despite my omnipresent knit hat) and stroll over to wish me well. It's the first time all day I feel a pinch of sadness, and I try to conjure the words I wrote to my team: *You do not need me there.*

Early in the second half we look bewildered and clumsy, out of step and off-kilter, and we're forced to play defense. The key is to contain Marta by swarming her at every opportunity. She finds an opening anyway, searing the ball toward our goal, where Hope saves us in the nick of time. Seven minutes left in regular time and we're suddenly commanding the action: a rocket by Carli (wide, damn it!); a shot by Angela Hucles (short!); and another by Amy Rodriguez that lands in their goalie's gloves. The clock's dwindled to zero: we're heading into overtime.

Seven minutes in, Carli fires one off, and their goalie dives a bit short—goal! Twenty-three minutes to gold. I watch through splayed fingers. Both sides are playing a game of tag, back and forth, back and forth, and despite the Brazilians' furious shooting, nothing finds the net. It's over and we win. *We won.* The diner patrons clap and shout, and I hop giddily on my good leg. I switch to my bad one, craving the physical pain—anything to distract from the melancholy rage of not being there on the field.

My phone buzzes. It's Dez, our equipment manager, calling from the locker room. "Hold on," he instructs, and I hear a roaring rush of screams and cheers, a celebration in absentia. I listen until I can't stand the sound anymore; I so badly wish my voice were in that chorus.

I hang up, terrified by the thought that they won without me.

11

APPRENTICE

In the weeks following the Olympics, I exist on two settings: numbed and tortured. Kara orchestrates an intense regimen of ice and elevation and compression, which I'm convinced will break my nascent cycle of injury. She sleeps on the couch with me, her feet by my head, and a few times per night I inadvertently wake her up with a swift kick to the temple. Without complaint, she rises and reboots the system, wrapping me in fresh ice and delivering another Vicodin. Occasionally, I creep back toward consciousness, coherent enough to drag my laptop toward me and power it on. Items I have no recollection of ordering begin showing up at my door: A five-piece patio set; a new mountain bike; a meat smoker as big as a bear. I do recall ordering a guitar, which becomes a new obsession, a way to channel my boundless energy with my fingers instead of my feet. Sometimes, when I'm lucky, I sleep through the night, and for those few hours my mind lets me believe it's all just a terrible dream.

I temporarily shed my aversion to crying, allowing myself to sob openly and without reservation, at least from the safety of my couch. These jags are about more than another failed romance and missing the Olympics; they're about my relationship with soccer, which, in a way, means they're about my relationship with myself. With past defeats I insisted on accepting all the blame: I wasn't fit enough; I wasn't prepared enough; I didn't want it enough, or I wanted other things more. For this Olympics, for the first time in my life, I don't believe those reasons. For the first time in my life I believe that soccer betrayed me, and I want to know why.

I am a novice at introspection, having spent my entire twenty-eight years focusing outward, throwing my energy into the air and seeing where it sticks. I am not sure where or how to start. Kara helps, burning incense and talking me through the basics of meditation. I try, feeling awkward and embarrassed, as if I'm on a first date with someone slightly out of my league. *Woman seeking woman who doesn't mind tobacco chew, extreme twin personalities, and long stretches of travel. A plus if you're bisexual and unable to commit!* Unsurprisingly, I can't shut up my mind; it's just as loud and obnoxious as my mouth. Kara tells me this is normal: the wandering mind is excavating negativity, pausing just long enough to yank those thoughts from the root. My dark thoughts have spread and twined like weeds. I wish I could hire a few freelance minds to give my own a helping hand.

I read Eckhart Tolle's *A New Earth* and find particular resonance in the sections about ego and seeking validation from within. Next is Gary Chapman's *The Five Love Languages,* which guides you to identify your preferred method of expressing and receiving affection, and I diagnose myself as a "giver." As soon as I had the means, I began giving outrageous gifts—to my nieces and nephews, my teammates, my girlfriends and friends. I give to make people happy, of course, but beneath that motivation there's another I am loath to admit: I give so that the recipients will like me. It's yet another subtle, insidious way I tell myself that I'm unworthy of genuine attention and love. I vow to work on that, to see what happens if I stop giving gifts.

When I'm not sitting perfectly still, working out my brain, I'm at physical therapy, finding my way back to my body. I'm soft and lopsided and every weighted step shoots a bolt of lightning through my bones. My right leg is a log; my left, a baseball bat whittled to its core. My doctor predicts my recovery will take a year, and mentally I chop that time in half: *Six months, max.* Every quad extension is as rigorous and painful as a dozen successive suicide runs. I push, add more weight, stretch, balance, walk, step, ice, compress, and repeat, cajoling the muscles back to life. I imagine myself returning to the field, sprinting its length, practicing set plays, feeling my head against the ball. Soccer has proved, to my surprise, that I am breakable, and I will find every piece I lost along the way.

At the end of September 2008, I'm well enough to travel to Manhattan for the draft of a new professional soccer league, Women's Professional Soccer (WPS), scheduled to launch in the spring. Despite the recession, the leagues' organizers are optimistic about its success. This time around there's a different business model, a grassroots approach in which seven teams operate and grow at the local level. I plan to play for the Washington Freedom, my old club team. A reporter for the *New York Times* asks me about missing the Olympics, and I reach for one of my new Zen mantras: "I wasn't devastated," I say, "because I accepted it when it happened. I try to live in the present."

In the first weeks of 2009, I pack up and head back east to Washington, D.C. My mala beads and Eckhart Tolle book both come with me.

On March 1, the first day of our preseason, I'm in the locker room with my teammates, getting ready for practice. Some are old friends but there are new faces, too, including a woman named Sarah Huffman to whom I'm immediately attracted. I laugh at myself for being so predictable; of course she has a flawless body, long hair, and could easily pass for straight. I worry, then, that maybe she *is* straight, and I'm already doomed. Despite my dismal track record, I hope she's at least bisexual, so I can convince her to give me a shot.

I have my answer soon enough, when I overhear her reading an e-mail from an ex-boyfriend. "Can you believe this guy?" she asks, and that conversation leads to another about visiting a friend in Turkey. I note that she says "friend," not girlfriend, as in, "I went to Turkey to visit my friend and we rode camels." Yet her tone is clear, and in some tacit way, her words are directed at me. *Why doesn't she just say "girlfriend"?* I think, but I'm relieved to know I'm not disqualified by my anatomy alone.

At practice, I'm constantly aware of where she's standing, and I maneuver myself to be next to her in drills. I'm nearby when she twists her leg awkwardly on the turf and goes down, flatly and swiftly, as if yanked by some unseen hand. She's wincing, clasping her right knee, and when her eyes open they meet mine. I'm standing over her, absolutely still, holding her gaze.

"You're going to be okay," I say, in the calmest tone I've ever used. "You don't know what's wrong. You don't know what you've done. You have to wait for the MRI. Just take this one step at a time, and believe me when I say you're going to be okay."

A few hours later the team hears the diagnosis: a torn ACL. That night, I plan to stop by her house. I assemble a care package, including DVDs, the Eckhart Tolle book, and a handwritten note telling her how sorry I am and that I know exactly how she's feeling. When I arrive, she has her leg up and is drinking a beer, surrounded by teammates. She loves the package and my note, and we all watch a few episodes of *The L Word,* a show about impossibly glamorous lesbians living in Los Angeles. I sit as close to Sarah as I can and do my best to make her laugh. Over the next few days we exchange long e-mails about injuries and the infuriating lack of control that accompanies them. I nearly beg: please tell me what I can do to help you get to the other side.

I have a chance on March 5, Sarah's birthday. We have off from practice the next morning, so a group of us go out to celebrate at the Eighteenth Street Lounge. I order her to sit and put her leg up while I fetch seven shots, each a different color of the rainbow. I help her to the bathroom, and when she emerges she grabs my hand, lacing her fingers through mine. I look at her, tighten my grip, but fail to make a move.

By the time she has her surgery, I'm spending more time at her place than my own. I make her coffee, fetch her books and painkillers, perch trays of food on her chest. I keep her company while she lies on the bed, her leg in a contraption that moves it automatically, bending and straightening. Her mom comes to visit, and she leaves us alone for long stretches so we can talk privately. Sarah opens her eyes as I squeeze in next to her.

"Do you want to be girlfriends with me?" she asks, the words slushy and slow.

"Yeah, I do," I say. "But can you ask me again when you're sober?"

Within the week I know that if I could marry her, I would.

12

HEAD CASE

The pendulum swings again, knocking me off balance, and I do nothing to stop it. I can blame it on external factors, if I so choose. Maybe soccer is literally going to my head. What else should I expect when I use it like a hammer? When I fall from the sky and land like a meteorite? When I refuse to stop even with staples in my scalp and blood in my eyes? When, at the end of my career, I'll agree to donate my brain for concussion research? Or I can acknowledge that I push the pendulum myself, and always have, ever since internalizing the idea that I have nothing to offer but my skill on the field. Give me that brutal, bruising pain that comes with moving; I'm not strong enough to handle the torture of being still.

I have few clear memories from 2009 and 2010, good or

bad. I remember a national team friendly against Canada, exactly one year and three days after breaking my leg. We happen to be playing in Rochester and my entire family is among the eighty-five hundred fans. Sarah surprises me by showing up, waving at me from the stands; it's the first time she's met my family, and I'm sure they'll love her as much as I do. We're tied, 0–0, and in the seventy-eighth minute I see my chance, shooting the ball past the right leg of the Canadian goalkeeper and into the net. It's my one hundredth career goal, and the crowd erupts, their cheers lapping at me, eroding the misery of the past year.

"I can't really describe the emotion," I say after the game, my platoon of nieces and nephews lining up to hug me. "It's been a long year, and to come home to score the hundredth goal in Rochester couldn't be more of a picture-perfect ending."

I remember a Washington Freedom game against the Boston Breakers in May 2010, an unremarkable, 0–0 matchup save for one spectacular collision: my nose against the opposing goalkeeper's arm. The crack is amplified inside my ears, and I feel the bone and cartilage slide across my face, ending up in the middle of my left cheek, a deformity so grotesque my teammates avert their eyes. When I have the gauze removed, Sarah—who has a lifelong fear of blood—is by my side, rocking back and forth, hands shielding her eyes so she doesn't faint from the sight. Four days later I send a triumphant group e-mail to select family and friends, including a close-up shot of my splinted nose and blackened eye:

"Ever since my nose break on Saturday I can safely say that the gauze that was just taken out of my nose was the most incredible thing that's ever happened!! The longest piece of gauze you could imagine. But now that I can breathe I am a whole new person."

I remember when the national team falters, losing to Mexico and facing the possibility of not qualifying for the 2011 World Cup in Germany. It's inconceivable that we lose to Mexico—our cumulative score against them in past games is 106–9—and even more unthinkable that we might be excluded from a major tournament. In order to right our course, we have to beat Costa Rica, and we do, 3–0. I score two of those goals, undeterred by a deep gash along my forehead, yet we're still not in the clear: next we have to beat Italy in the playoff series. Losing means we're staying home.

I remember the media attention surrounding our potential defeat and humiliation, and how it feels deliberately and sharply unfair. I take the opportunity to share my observations with the *New York Times*. "The irony of the whole thing," I say, "is that when the U.S. men win, they get the coverage, but when the U.S. women lose, we get the coverage. . . . The joke among us is that we planned it this way and that we knew this was the only way to get the coverage that we think we deserve." I tuck this feeling away to examine later, knowing it extends far beyond the tone of newspaper articles, affecting every aspect of our game.

I remember when the WPS begins sinking, once again failing to re-create the buzz and excitement that follow World Cup and Olympic years. Franchises lose millions of dollars and begin dropping out, one by one. Toward the end of 2010, the Washington Freedom's owners sell the team to a Boca Raton–based entrepreneur named Dan Borislow, who rechristens it "magicJack" after his prized invention: a USB-plug-in device that enables users to make unlimited Web calls from their phones. He recruits me and a few other high-profile members of the national team: Hope Solo, Pearcie, Shannon Boxx. Sarah joins, too, and we move together to Florida.

I like Dan and the feeling is mutual; he sees himself in me—loud and unfiltered, prone to all-night revelry and vulgar proclamations. I admire his willingness to blurt out what others are thinking, his steadfast trust in his own instincts. He invites us all to test-drive his collection of luxury cars, my guilty pleasure, and ensconces us in condos with lavish amenities: a private theater, a spa, a rooftop pool. He takes us to Easter brunch at Mar-Al-Lago, where we feast on lobster and caviar. At dinner, he buys endless hundred-dollar bottles of wine and bluntly inquires about our sex lives. "Which one of you is the giver and which one is the receiver?" he asks one teammate, and then turns to another. "Why have you never had a sexual relationship with a woman?" During practice, he occasionally deems us "fucking idiots." When a teammate inquires how he'd like to be addressed—Dan, Mr. Borislow, or Coach—he has a different idea, instructing her to call him "Daddy."

His boorish patter belies his remarkably progressive attitude toward women's soccer. In e-mails to *ESPN the Magazine,* he touches upon issues I don't yet have the courage to discuss out loud. "Why is it okay that the athletes who represent our country the best should be paid wages that leave them at the poverty level?" he asks. "I would never pay someone who is best in their field these types of ridiculous wages. It would be embarrassing. We should not have a pro league in this country unless they get paid real wages." He backs up his bluster with action, giving us all a significant raise, and announces, "It is not okay to treat women like crap and abuse them. . . . The women to a large degree have accepted this treatment."

There are many, many nights out with Dan that I don't remember at all.

I remember going back to Los Angeles in the off-season, bringing Sarah with me, double-dating with Kara and her girlfriend. One morning, out of earshot of the others, Kara corners me. She speaks to me in a voice I don't recognize, accusing me of things I am not ready to accept. I am drinking too much; I am numbing too much; I am wandering into a dangerous space. The situation has escalated since she first admonished me, back in 2007, to work on my responsible self.

"You've ruined my day," I tell her. "I'm going to the beach."

For now, we leave it at that. I soon turn back to soccer, the drug I have no choice but to take.

13

G.O.A.T.

During the countdown to the 2011 World Cup, I break my strict, career-long rule and drink during camp—not excessively, but enough to dilute any thoughts that drift away from soccer. One thought I can't suppress is that my body, day by day and degree by degree, is becoming a lesser version of itself. Every part of it has to be addressed, piecemeal, before I make it to the field. The shaky ankle requires wrapping, and the Achilles tendon needs a combination of electric stimulation and ultrasound therapy, a process so prolonged and intense it seems to deaden my tissue. At night I wear a splint that dorsiflexes my foot, and in the morning I need to pump my ankle for a half hour just to be able to stand. I alternate between wearing cleats and a boot to keep my ankle in a set position. My leg bones can feel the rain before it falls. I'm newly thirty-one, and for the first time I'm wondering how much longer I can play this game.

But now, in Germany, I have to talk myself through the tweaks and pangs, relegate them to the sidelines. I begin the tournament in a scoring drought, shots deflecting off the post and headers veering wide, an embarrassment underscored by my teammates' unspoken concern: *What's wrong with Wambach?* During our final group match game against Sweden, the ball soars toward me and I vie for position. Planting my legs, I rear my torso back like a slingshot, snap forward and connect with the knob of my shoulder, shoving the ball in for a goal. *Nothing's wrong with Wambach,* I think. *I'm back, at least for now.*

We move on to Dresden, where we face Brazil in the quarterfinals. I recall how the Brazilians not only trounced us in 2007, but danced and sang in our hotel lobby as we entered, inconsolable. There's a chance the scene may be repeated—we're again staying in the same hotel as our rivals—and I gather the younger players around to tell them the story. "I would give up every goal I've ever scored to win this World Cup," I say. "You have to be willing to give up everything." Silently I add an addendum: I'd give up everything because this might be the last World Cup I ever see.

From the field the spectators seem miniature, with candlestick arms and pinpoint faces. My parents, siblings, Are, Dena,

Kara, and Sarah sit amid thousands of people who are eager for us to lose. The July heat hangs heavy and low, whisking up a sheen of sweat before I even start to move. Seventy-four seconds in and we're on the board, albeit accidentally, when Brazilian defender Daiane deflects the ball into her own net. Ugly, but I'll take it. There's a chorus of long and lusty boos; no one likes Americans.

I get my first shot, challenging the Brazilian goalkeeper inside the box, but it swerves wide. Twelve minutes later Brazil comes to life, with Marta prancing fifty yards down the field only for her shot to sail over the bar. The crowd swells into a wave, standing and tossing their hands, hoping to fuel Brazil's momentum.

We're going back and forth, up and down, and suddenly I'm airborne, a body on top of me, collapsing into a tangle of limbs as we slam into the ground. I twist my head to see the Brazilian defender Aline. She gets a booking—a yellow card from the referee—for the tackle, and then Marta earns one of her own by yapping her dissent. By halftime we're still up, 1–0. Beneath the wrappings, beneath the shots and pills and all the deliberate numbness, my body and mind are both screaming.

Pearcie and Pia do their usual thing in the locker room, dispensing strategy and sense, and then I do mine in the huddle: patriotism, camaraderie, grit, an expletive. On the count of three, we chant "Oosa, Oosa, Oosa, Ah!" and we're back on the field.

In the sixty-fifth minute, Rachel Buehler leaps sideways

at Marta, taking her down, with the Brazilian performing her usual theatrics, flipping and writhing. The ruse works. Rachel gets a red card—instant ejection—and she leaves the field distraught. Later, she tells me she watched on a thirteen-inch TV in the doping room, crying the whole time, sure she had lost it for us. For the duration of the game we'll have just ten players on the field.

The Brazilian player Cristiane lines up to take the penalty kick, but Hope launches herself in its path and stops it. Wait—what the hell is this? The referee makes an insane call, claiming Hope moved off her line, and orders a do-over. This time, Marta steps up. She kicks one way while Hope jumps the other, and the game is tied, 1–1. The crowd turns, booing the referees and scowling at the Brazilians, and now we're the good guys, the underdogs. Chants of *USA! USA!* filter down to the field. By the end of regulation, the game remains tied. We're going into overtime.

In the ninety-second minute, Marta scores on a set play at such an absurdly severe angle that I can't help but admire the shot. Brazil takes the lead. *That's going to be that,* I think. *That's how soccer goes. If you score in overtime, that's usually the game. We're still down a man, and everything is against us.* Then my heart responds to my mind, raising an objection: *No! We can still do this. It's not over yet.*

We have to keep pushing regardless, acting as though we believe we have a chance. We hustle, we take our spots, we try to execute a set play but fail. Wasted moves, wasted energy. I am heaving, sprinting as fast as I ever have and not quite getting where I need to be; if only I could detach my leg or head or both and hurl them at the ball—anything to push it closer to the goal. I reach it, finally, and manage a weak kick that skids low and wide of the post.

Now I'm getting angry. I want the ball to go where I want it to go; I want my body to do what it's being asked. I want this to be as effortless for me as it's always been. And just like that, my body talks back, louder than I've ever heard it speak: *Make me. I dare you.*

I accept the challenge—I've never known how to turn one down—and scream to my teammates: "If we just get one chance, I know we'll score!"

Marta seems to be in three places at once, sailing and swooping. We are stretched thin and exhausted, trailing limply in her wake. Time is dwindling: 113th minute, 118th, 120th. The final whistle could blow any second. Brazil's Erika goes down, writhing in pain over a phantom tackle, a classic ploy to run down the clock. A stretcher is called for, and she hops on and off it, miraculously ready to play again. Another waterfall of boos from the crowd. But her theatrics give us time to move the ball forward.

We're ping-ponging it across and up the field: Pearcie to Ali Krieger to Carli Lloyd, who takes a bunch of touches. *What are you doing?* I think, and yell, "Carli, play direct! Don't kick it wide!" My ear is anticipating the sound of the whistle, signaling our loss, our time to pack up and go home. Carli plays the ball to Megan Rapinoe. I'm not sure if she sees me, but she's running toward me, and I know exactly what she'll do next: look up and bomb it into the box. She does, the ball flying from her laces into a magnificent arc, stretching higher and higher . . .

I creep into position, waiting to pounce. My mind gives me a last-second pep talk: *Please don't miss. It would be the most epic failure in the history of the game if you miss.*

The reflexive memory of every past goal is packed into this second, informing the way I move—leaping off my right leg, slanting shoulders forward, matching the ball to my hairline, as inevitable as a puzzle piece finding its slot. That sweet, familiar second of darkness.

I open my eyes and know: I didn't miss. It's the latest goal ever scored in a World Cup.

I celebrate as flamboyantly as any Brazilian, running saucer-eyed toward my teammates and sliding on the turf, stopping myself just before I reach cement. When I pop up they're all around me, bouncing and slapping my back. Pinoe leaps into my arms and I carry her for a few steps. It's not over, but we're close. *We got this,* I think, and we do: Five penalty kicks later, the board is lit with the final score: USA 5, Brazil 3.

We win the battle but lose the war, falling in the final to Japan, which is still recovering from that spring's earthquake and tsunami; I reason that their country needs the win more than ours does. I also take the loss as a personal message: soccer still feeds me in a way nothing else does, and we are not yet finished with each other.

14

ROMANTIC

Despite our second-place finish at the World Cup, America's interest in soccer surges to a degree unseen since the era of the 99ers. I revel in the postgame reports describing celebrities' reactions to our win over Brazil. "Wambach!!!!" comedian Seth Meyers tweeted after my late goal. "Wowwwwww! Goal was amazing," added NFL star Kerry Rhodes. LeBron James, P. Diddy, and Gabrielle Union all chimed in with their compliments and congratulations. The team is invited to appear on the *Today* show, *Good Morning America,* and *The Late Show with David Letterman.*

For me, the most meaningful assessment comes from Mia Hamm. "How did you do that?" she asks. "That was the most amazing thing I've ever witnessed." Dan Borislow, who watched from the stands, echoes that sentiment, telling me it was the "most impressive athletic play to ever happen in the history of women's soccer." Random people tell me they remember exactly where they were when they saw my goal, a phenomenon I thought applied only to assassinations and sensational trial verdicts. My agent's phone buzzes with endorsement offers. I sense a pivotal turning point for soccer; maybe the women's game will now find the attention and respect it deserves.

When I return to Florida, I'm met with a hard dose of reality: my magicJack club team is about to implode. While the national players were in Germany, the rest of the team filed a grievance against Dan Borislow, citing "inappropriate statements and conduct toward his players, and players' fear of improper retaliation by Mr. Borislow based on their grievance." After a loss to Boston, Dan sent a blistering e-mail: "I didn't play this shitty game, you did." He also threatened them with "suicide runs"—a mile in only five minutes—and insisted they took scalding Jacuzzi baths before practice. My old teammate Briana Scurry quit. While the WPS investigates the grievance, Dan is banned from the sidelines, and I'm named the player-coach.

Attendance in the beginning of the season was dismal, rarely exceeding one thousand spectators. After the World Cup, the numbers increase exponentially, culminating in a crowd of 15,404 when we head north to play the Western New York Flash at their home stadium—*my* home stadium, with my family filling rows and rows of bleachers. It's a single-game attendance record for the league, and I address the cheering crowd at halftime, apologizing for riding the bench to rest my Achilles tendon. They chant my name and wave bobbleheads of my likeness. Our season ends the following month after a playoff loss to Philadelphia, and even with the renewed enthusiasm in soccer, I'm worried about the future of the league—especially when the WPS board of directors, citing ongoing issues with Dan, votes to terminate the magicJack team.

In the fall, Sarah and I move back to Hermosa Beach and I start to plan my proposal. Our commonalities brought us together, but I think our differences will make us last, safeguarding against my extremes. We each know our roles and play them well. I cook elaborate feasts, piling the counters with pots and pans, and she cleans up every last crumb. I shop with abandon and she waits for sales. I scatter and she organizes. I bounce from interest to interest, and she takes her time in both adopting and abandoning hobbies. She is a passionate but even-keeled warrior who's not afraid to challenge me. I am happy, happier than I've ever been, which gives me a newfound appreciation for those long, deep trenches of depression. Without them, the happiness would be duller, leached of color and noise.

I have a ring designed by my family's longtime jeweler in Rochester, and the end result is perfect: a cushion-cut diamond flanked by smaller stones, set in platinum. While I'm at it, I order two wedding rings for Sarah, simple bands of round diamonds. Put together, it looks like the center stone is floating on a sparkling pillow of diamonds. I decide to pop the question around the holidays, and until then I mark the passing time on my calendar. I plan each moment meticulously and daydream about how it will unfold, Intense Abby and Chill Abby both in their element.

For Christmas, we fly to Dallas to visit her parents. I remain intensely traditional in some ways; there are lessons from my mother I can't unlearn. I will never get a tattoo, or want my partner to have one. I'll never find out the sex of my children before they're born. And I believe that if you intend to propose, it's respectful to ask your partner's parents for their blessing. Now, in Dallas, I know it's the only chance I'm going to have, and I'm buzzing with nerves. After dinner, and numerous glasses of wine, I find them in the kitchen. The three of us are alone; Sarah has gone out with her sister. Her mother is gathering plates and her father is washing dishes, hands plunged into the sink.

Pulling the ring out of my pocket, I say the words I've been practicing in my head: I'm in love with their daughter, and I want nothing more than to spend the rest of my life with her. I will honor and cherish her always, and take care of her, and it would mean everything if I could have their blessing.

Time passes. It could be a minute, five, ten; I'm too petrified to count. Everyone is on pause. Me, standing with the ring pinched between my fingers. Sarah's mother, halfway to the sink, balancing a pyramid of plates. Her father, hands motionless beneath running water. *Drip, drip, drip.*

At last, her mother punctures the moment. "Oh, wow," she says, and the words shake her dad into action. "Oh, wow," he repeats, and adds, "I was not expecting that question."

I smile, but I'm shrinking inside. My mind rummages for ways to justify this reaction. I know her father worries that Sarah lives in my shadow, soccer-wise, and he (understandably) wants her to feel independent and be able to support herself. And while I know it's not *me,* per se—her parents have always loved me—I suspect they'd hoped that when Sarah settled down, the needle on the bisexuality wheel would be pointing toward "man." There's no denying it would be an easier life, but, I argue silently, not necessarily a happier one.

Finally, her mother speaks again. "Oh, we're so thrilled!" she exclaims, and rushes to embrace me. I love her even more for lying just to make me comfortable.

The day after Christmas it's time to launch phase 2, which I've been planning for months. I've arranged for a group of our closest friends to meet in Breckenridge, Colorado, for a few nights of New Year's revelry. We've rented a huge cabin set high in the mountains, and Sarah and I are there to greet each new arrival. There's food and wine and more wine, but not so much that we can't rally for a group hike the next day. While Sarah is getting ready, I gather all our friends and whisper my instructions. "Listen," I say. "At some point on this hike, when we come to a really steep hill, just stop and say, 'Hey, I'm tired. I'm going to go back.' And one by one you guys will haul ass down. And when we get back, we're going to have a hell of an engagement party." They agree, and we head out.

Breckenridge is ninety-six hundred feet above sea level, and within twenty minutes all of us are gasping, our breath turning into smoke against the chilled air. One by one our friends profess exhaustion, turn around, and head back down to the cabin, until Sarah and I are alone at the top of a hill. The sky looks made of antique lace, draping down on snow-dusted mountains and winding through the trees, and it ribbons around us, framing the moment.

From my backpack I pull out a photo album titled "Life As We Knew It." Every picture I'd taken of us since the beginning of our relationship is arranged in careful order, accompanied by funny or sentimental or romantic captions. The last page reads: "I just have one more question." When she turns around I'm on bended knee, holding the ring aloft.

I tell her all the reasons I want to marry her, keeping just one to myself: I know she will never let me get too far gone.

She says yes.

15

HERO

Before I come out of hibernation for the Olympics, before Intense Abby steps forward and asserts herself, Sarah tells me she has a surprise.

"Hey," she says. "April 8 is the third anniversary of our first date. We're going somewhere."

We drive my Jeep twenty minutes from Hermosa to Long Beach, the wind cooling our faces as quickly as the sun warms them, everything in harmony. She's packed a picnic basket, but I'm not allowed to peek inside. I attempt to guess our destination and she merely smiles in response. We pull into a heliport, where a two-seater helicopter is waiting, and the pilot lifts us up and lands us in Catalina.

Taking my hand, she leads me to a golf cart and we drive

around town, teetering through the narrow streets and stopping at a wedge of land overlooking the ocean. She spreads out a blanket and arranges our picnic: fruit, cheese, champagne. After a toast, she retrieves a wooden box and instructs me to open it. I do, and find a series of letter blocks, arranged in a sentence: WILL YOU MARRY ME? I look up, shocked, and see she's holding a ring: a thick platinum band studded with diamonds, exactly what I've always wanted.

As we embrace, a thought occurs to me, and I have to voice it: "Did you ask my mom and dad?"

"Yeah," she says, and takes me through the moment. After I proposed at Christmas, she called my parents in New York and said she had a question to ask relating to Abby, to our relationship. She knew the question would make my parents uncomfortable and she began crying and fumbling her words, until my mother took pity and spoke first. "Don't cry," she said. "We love you, and as long as you're happy and as long as it's something Abby wants, we want you both to be happy."

I am happy—as happy about my parents' approval as I am about the proposal—and I settle into the moment, wishing I could stretch it into the future with a guarantee that it will never snap back.

After that trip, I meet the national team for training camp in Florida. I am motivated, fully aware that this may be my last Olympics, and despite its age and ailments my body still does what I ask of it, falling back into its familiar routine:

First, get up at 8 A.M. and immediately pee in a cup to check hydration levels. Dawn Scott, our strength and conditioning coach (and quasi–team therapist), then calculates how many hydrating solutions I need, and I get down to the business of drinking them as quickly as I can. More than sprints, more than weights, more than dieting, more than ninety minutes of nonstop scrimmaging, I hate drinking water. In fact, I list it as one of my personal failings, deserving of a proper title with capital letters: "Terrible Drinker of Water." But I slog through it, feeling as though my organs are swimming inside me.

Next, eat breakfast (two fried eggs, hot sauce, toast) and drink coffee, thereby negating the hard work I've done to hydrate. Read the paper, do a crossword puzzle. Tape my ankle and pull on my boot—my Achilles tendon is still in agony—and head to the field, slipping on my cleats as soon as I arrive. Start warm-up laps, jogging back and forth across the field, catching up with my teammates. What did they do the night before? What are they reading? (On my nightstand at the time is *Quiet: The Power of Introverts in a World That Can't Stop Talking*—an attempt to better communicate with shyer players.) What TV show are they watching? Are they still fighting with their husband or boyfriend or girlfriend? If I'm feeling especially chatty, or if the collective mood is subdued, I'll say something shocking to shake things up. "How many times per week do the rest of you have sex?" I'll ask, or describe, in detail, the suppurating wound on my shin—one of the joys of playing on field turf.

Then on to drills, set plays, batting the ball with my head, over and over again. Hit the weight room for supersets and plyometrics. Afterward, I worry about increasing the girth of my legs; like every other girl on the planet, I've studied my body in the mirror and thought, *My thighs are huge.*

On to the recovery room, finally, where I pull on compression pants and sit still for a half hour, waiting for the swelling to deflate. To unwind, I play video games—soccer, football, and poker—and then call Sarah. I want to hear about her day and imagine I'm there; no event is irrelevant, no detail too mundane. *Four more months until the Olympics,* I tell myself, *and then I can get back to my life.*

Our next training camp is in Princeton, New Jersey. The same routine, but with one key difference: Kara is back with the team, working as our sports therapist. Our relationship has been strained since she confronted me about my drinking before last year's World Cup. One night, after I leave the recovery room, she asks to speak to me privately, and I follow her into her hotel room.

"What the fuck?" she says. "Things are weird between us, ever since I said something to you. They feel inauthentic." She asks questions: Do I understand how difficult it was for her to confront me? Especially since I've made a habit of surrounding myself with people who would rather have fun with me than be *real* with me? Especially since I can be prickly when I hear something I don't want to believe?

"Look," I say. "I love you, but I don't trust you."

Wearing my C.Y.P. uniform, feeling proud that day because I crushed it on the court.

(Photo courtesy of the author)

Kamikaze team picture in the McQuaid gym. After scoring twenty-seven goals in three games, I was asked to join the boys' soccer league.

(Photos courtesy of the author)

I was excited to join the U-20 National Team. When we arrived at camp no one was expecting us. As a consolation they let me try on my uniform.
(Photo courtesy of the author)

In 1996, my Region 1 ODP team went to Beijing to compete. This was the first time I experienced a completely different culture. I would learn to accept that I would never understand time zones. *(Photo courtesy of the author)*

In disbelief after Mercy High lost the New York State championship game in the second overtime to Massapequa, 1997. *(Courtesy* Democrat and Chronicle*/D&C Digital)*

With Kelly O'Neill and Gina Montesano—my high school teammates in both basketball and soccer—at the Empire State Games. *(Photo courtesy of the author)*

Congratulating Mia Hamm after scoring a goal on China's National Women's Soccer Team, 2004. *(Photo by Don Emmert/AFP/Getty Images)*

LEFT: Warming up before a friendly game prior to the 2007 World Cup.
RIGHT: After I scored my 100th goal in Rochester, New York, 2009.

(Photos courtesy of the author)

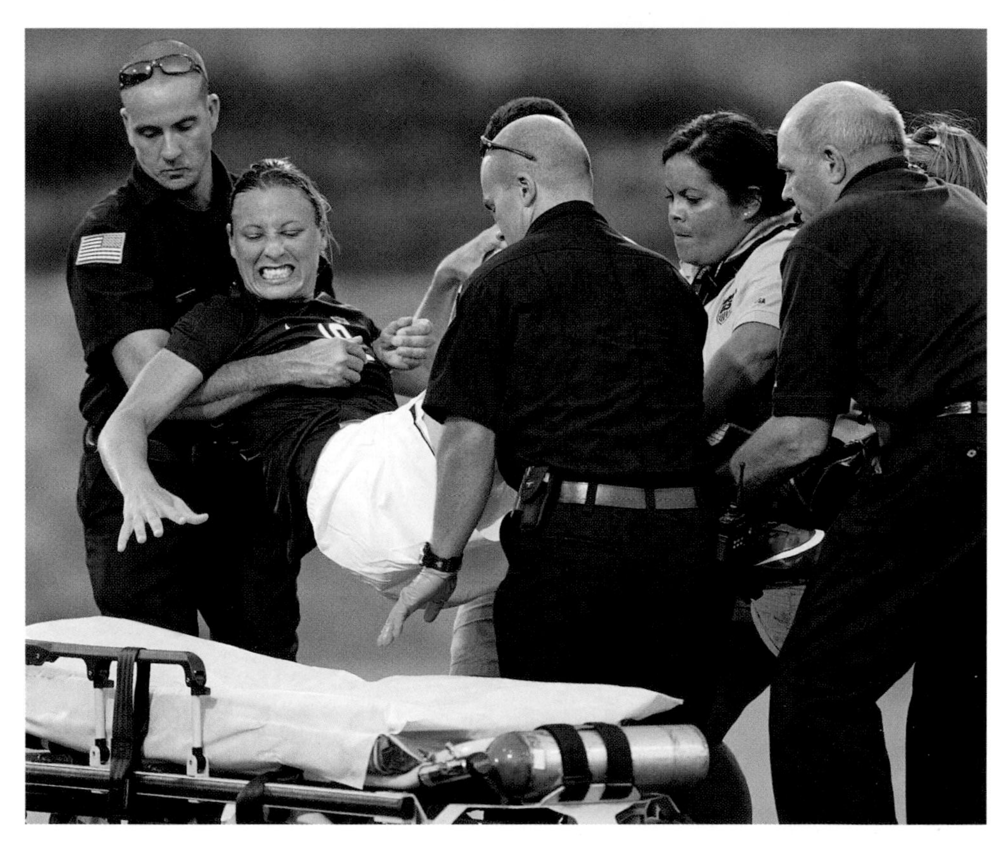

Being taken off the field after a hard hit during the game against Brazil in 2008.

(Photo: U-T San Diego/ZUMAPRESS.com)

A header at the Algarve Cup in Portugal, 2008.
(Photo: M. Stahlschmidt/SSP © 2016)

Starting IX for a friendly match against Canada in Rochester, New York, 2009.
(Photo courtesy of the author)

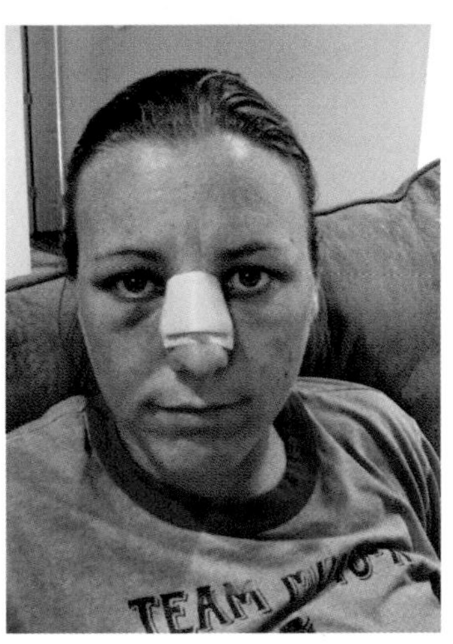

Celebrating with teammates Alex Morgan and Megan Rapinoe after scoring in the first half of the women's quarterfinal match during the London 2012 Olympic Games. I was always too big to jump on anyone, so I was often the one being jumped on. *(Christopher Hanewinckel/USA Today Sports)*

After breaking my nose during the 2010 exhibition match against Ireland and having it fixed surgically. Possibly the most excruciating injury I've had in my career. *(Photo courtesy of the author)*

Tired but elated after defeating Japan 2-1 to win the Women's Soccer gold medal match at the London 2012 Olympic Games.
(Photo by Julian Finney/Getty Images)

After I scored my 159th goal (against South Korea, 2013) to bypass Mia Hamm for the most-goals-scored record. *(Photo By Don Emmert/AFP/Getty Images)*

After I became the all-time goal-scoring leader in international competitions, Nike surprised me with my very own cleat. I was shocked and awed by the detail they put into making this one-of-a-kind shoe. *(Photo by Nike)*

LEFT: Singing the national anthem at the CONCACAF Women's Championship against Costa Rica at PPL Park. We won 6-0. *(Derik Hamilton/USA Today Sports)*
RIGHT: Red carpet at the 2015 Time 100 Gala at Lincoln Center in New York City.
(Photo by Andrew Toth/FilmMagic/Getty Images)

My entire family came out to support me for my 2015 retirement game in New Orleans.
(Photo courtesy of the author)

During the 2015 World Cup, friends and family got to come and meet players post-game. I was always grateful to get away from the stress of a big tournament.
(Photo courtesy of the author)

After scoring against Nigeria during the 2015 WWC. *(Photo: L. Benedict/SSP © 2016)*

After winning the 2015 World Cup final, I went over to Sarah and whispered, "I did it, WE did it." "Kiss me!" she said. *(Associated Press)*

Taking a lap after the World Cup Final. One of the best moments was spotting my family in the stands. *(Photo by Dennis Grombkowski/Getty Images)*

Oh, hey, Mr. President, would you mind taking a selfie with us? At the White House, presenting President Barack Obama with an honorary team jersey. *(Geoff Burke/USA Today Sports)*

Pre-game hug with my idol, teammate, and friend, Mia Hamm, before my last game in a national team jersey. *(Photo by Dan Levy)*

Victory Tour 2015 goodbye to all my fans. I love you all, forever. *(Photo by Christian Petersen/ Getty Images)*

I was honored to have the opportunity to stump for Hillary Clinton in 2016 and talk about the importance of voting.
(Photo by Scott Eisen/Getty Images)

After the World Cup win, I traveled the country meeting with the brightest minds to talk about equality. Apple CEO Tim Cook is such a beautiful soul.
(Photo by Dan Levy)

She aims her next words with precision. "You don't trust me because I care about you?"

I'm stolid and impassive. "No," I said. "I have to work my way back to trusting you again."

I turn and leave. I know the conversation is just beginning, but right now I'm not able to hear another word.

I'm in England, at the Olympics, in a place I haven't been for eight years. I remember how miserable I was back in 2008, laid up with my broken leg, having to summon every last leadership instinct to stop myself from flying to China—to stop myself from making it all about me. I am feeling strong and ready and, most of all, *present,* steeped in every moment, all my focus and energy on the task ahead. Before the flight, a reporter asked me what my expectations were for the games.

"Based on the fact that we have so many fans now, and so many people pulling for us," I said, "for me, it's gold or bust."

My agent, Dan Levy, was standing beside me. "Did you really just say that?" he asked.

"Sure did."

He laughed. "Well, you'd better bring that gold home, then."

"I got this," I told him. "We got this."

And now, on the field against France, I can see that we do. Although we start off tentative and shaky, allowing two goals in the first sixteen minutes, we push back, finding our groove. I score the first U.S. goal of the game: a corner kick from Pinoe that ricochets perfectly off my head. Three more goals—two from Alex Morgan and one from Carli—and we win our first game, 4–2. We win our second, too, against Colombia, during which I get sucker-punched in my right eye. Afterward I tweet a close-up picture of my shiner: "Thanks for all the well wishes. Eye is healing fine." #reverse smokeyeye #notcool.

We win next against North Korea—my busted eye doesn't prevent me from scoring the game's lone goal—and nine of us clasp hands and celebrate by attempting old-school popping and waving, undulating our arms from the beginning of the chain to the end. We win another against New Zealand, with a goal from me and one from Sydney Leroux, a new player I've started to mentor. She wears an expression of joyous shock, as if she can't quite believe what she's done, and I recognize what I've never had: a pure love for the game, so real and intense she'd even play alone.

Our semifinal game, against Canada, is later named by the *Globe and Mail* as "the greatest game of women's soccer ever played." The game is rough and dirty before it even begins; John Herdman, the Canadian head coach, accuses us of "illegal tactics" and singles me out specifically, citing my header against France off a corner kick. I recognize his motives: he wants to gain an early advantage by shaking our confidence and preemptively influencing the referees. Despite myself I have to admire his cunning; I understand the willingness to do whatever it takes to win.

From the opening whistle, the play is a brutal spectacle of

tackles, shirt pulling, elbowing, jostling, and one deliberate stomp on Carli's head. The crowd boos Tobin Heath when she (fairly) wins a tussle. I'm keeping my eye on Christine Sinclair, a forward who's neck and neck with me in the race to score the most international goals; as of this moment, she has 140 to my 142. I've called her "the most underrated player on the planet" and in the twenty-third minute she proves it, spinning and twisting through our back line and finding herself free in the box. She curls a shot to Hope's right and hits the net with conviction (141 to my 142, now) giving the Canadians momentum as we brawl our way toward halftime. We haven't lost to Canada in eleven years, and I don't intend to let them break that streak.

My body does what it does best, mauling and blocking and barreling through. On a header attempt I'm called for climbing on a Canadian defender. Two minutes later I try again, leaping high and forward and aiming my head at the ball, which soars just past the post. At halftime, it's still 1–0, and we gather in the locker room and reiterate a team vow: There is no way in hell we're losing to Canada. There is no way in hell we're going home without making it to the final and winning gold.

The second half starts off as turbulently as the first, with frantic back and forth in the midfield and jostling in the box, elbows stabbing and hands pulling and heads banging. I launch myself skyward, careening toward space, slamming the ball high with my chest—too high, it turns out, and I watch it loop over the bar. We execute set piece after set piece with me as the fulcrum—the vital part of the machine that makes it click and whirl—but the Canadians have studied me, anticipating my next move before I make it. The ball eludes me. Pinoe is luckier, or maybe less scrutinized, and scores with a gorgeous, unlikely corner kick in the fifty-third minute. We're tied, 1–1, and the play on both sides accelerates, the ball zigzagging up and down the field. In six wild minutes three goals are scored—another by Sinclair (142 to 142, now), another by Pinoe, and yet another by Sinclair; I care less about her temporary lead in our goal race than I do about the Canadians' lead in the game, 3–2.

With seventeen minutes left in regulation, I notice their goalkeeper trying to stall, taking longer than the allowed six seconds to dropkick the ball back into play. Within earshot of the referee, I start counting, making it all the way to ten. The referee notices but does nothing. When their goalkeeper stalls again, I resume my counting: One, two, three . . . and the referee blows her whistle for a six-second violation—a rare, nearly unprecedented call. I take a penalty kick, tying the game at 3–3. In the 123rd minute, Carli passes to Heather O'Reilly, who crosses to Alex; she rockets up and bats her head against the ball, sending it high over her defender and into the net.

We win, 4–3, and I find Alex in the thrashing pile of teammates. "I love you," I scream at her. "I think I'm in love with you in this moment."

Meanwhile, Twitter blows up, condemning me for counting out loud to the referee.

"Dear FIFA," reads one tweet, "please investigate Abby Wambach for unsporting behaviour in attempting to influence the referee's decision."

Another: "Sorry, I will not be moved on this: Abby Wambach should be ashamed. It's the Olympics, remember."

And my personal favorite: "I want to get a punching bag, paste Abby Wambach's face on it and work out."

I tell reporters I regret nothing: "You can say it's gamesmanship, you can say it's smart, but I'm a competitor. We needed to get a goal." Besides, I add, the incident rallied Canadians behind their team, and women's sports need as much support as they can get, no matter the source or reason.

On August 8, a few hours before we're to meet Japan in the gold medal game, I open my e-mail and find a message from Kara. The subject line reads "T," signaling the next installment of our private game: Pick a letter for the other person, explain the meaning behind your choice, and exhort them to rise to the occasion.

The body says:

> I pick the letter 'T' for you.
>
> We hit a rough patch this year . . .
>
> Shit came up and stared us both in the face. It was ugly and it was uncomfortable.
>
> The letter T
>
> Just before we left L.A. for this trip you looked at me in your living room, right after we sang the Lana Del Rey song together . . . You said, 'Kara, the way I've been with you

doesn't work for me anymore.' You told me how important it was to you that I was a part of your life.

The letter T

How is it that an ugly caterpillar climbs itself onto a tree limb, spins a cocoon, and completely disintegrates itself—only to emerge a butterfly with exquisite colors that can take flight?

Transformation. That's how.

From my heart space to yours . . .

Thank you.

Get it done tonight.

—K.

Immediately I write back: "T it is."

And in that moment, I mean it.

We get it done in Wembley Stadium before a booming crowd of 80,203, just a few hundred shy of capacity—the largest audience for women's soccer since the 1999 World Cup final at the Rose Bowl. My support system—parents, siblings, Kara, Are, his mother Dena, Sarah, and assorted other family and friends—are all there, thanks to Dan Borislow, who paid for their flights and hotels. I am getting chances but can't convert, my headers soaring wide or falling short. But Carli comes through twice and we finish 2–1. My skin is still wet from sprays of champagne when I bow my head to accept the gold medal.

I don't yet want to face the possibility that it might be the last one I wear. I give interviews in which I talk about my successful tournament—five goals in six games—and field questions about my injuries. They're under control, I insist, helped by a rigorous regimen of ice baths, compression stockings, and my boot-shaped night splint, and I will be on this field as long as my body allows. "If I can get fully well and feel good, I want to be a part of this team. I think I'm a lifer."

A week later, back home in Hermosa Beach, I wear the medal out for a walk with Sarah and two friends. It's early afternoon, and I've been drinking since I woke up, and we stop for pizza and more beer at Paisanos on the pier. Passersby recognize me and notice the medal, and I stop for photos and high fives, laughing and slinging my arm around strange shoulders. Someone with a camera approaches, zooming in on the beer in my hand and following me as I leave. Only later, after it's uploaded, do I realize that he works for TMZ.

"How's it going, Abby?" the cameraman calls to me. "Congratulations!"

IT'S ABBY WAMBACH, blares the voiceover in the finished video, WHO LED THE U.S. WOMEN'S SOCCER TEAM TO GOLD GLORY!

"Is this an official diet?" the cameraman asks.

"This is past the diet, yeah!" I say, the words struggling to escape my mouth. "Let's be real, like, it's pizza, so . . ."

AND YOU KNOW WHAT GOES GREAT WITH

PIZZA? the voiceover intones, flashing a GIF of a drooling Homer Simpson. BEER!

The video cuts to the TMZ offices, where a woman staffer says the obvious: "I guess she's been drinking." Another staffer adds, "She was *wasted* . . . she was not only wasted, she was *day-drinking*." A third chimes in: "She was partying the entire afternoon." A fourth has mercy: "Which is fine. It's a beautiful, hot day out."

AND SHE'S EARNED IT, the voiceover concludes. ABBY'S AN AMERICAN HERO, DAMMIT!

Sarah saves me, wrapping her arm around my back and leading me away.

The video is watched more than two million times, and the vast majority of commenters think it's hilarious and don't judge me at all. For years I think it's hilarious, too, until suddenly I don't.

16

WIFE

We are going to have the best life. Our dreams are lining up, just waiting for us to claim them. As predicted, the WPS league has folded, but a new one has sprung up in its place: the National Women's Soccer League (NWSL), and Sarah and I both play for the Western New York Flash. We live in Buffalo, an hour from my family, and we both hate it: the cold, the smallness of the town. I remind her that the season is short—just four months—and we'll move on. We have faith that something new and exciting will always be waiting for us, as long as we know where to look.

At age thirty-two, my career has reached its pinnacle: I've been named FIFA Women's World Player of the Year, edging out my teammate Alex Morgan and Marta, my perennial rival from the Brazilian team. I score my 159th goal, breaking Mia Hamm's record for the most goals by any player, male or female. It happens in June 2013, during a game against South Korea; a corner kick finds my head and I punch it in, sure and smooth, my instant amnesia telegraphing my triumph. I am grateful to my teammates, who worked mightily to get me the ball, and when reporters inquire about my next goal, I tell them this: "I want to give more assists to Alex Morgan, so she can break my record." And I mean it: there would be no greater tribute than being surpassed.

For the first time, I have fleeting thoughts about what life might look like after retirement: How I will I support myself, and Sarah, and our family? What can an aging athlete with an unfinished degree in "Leisure Management" do? I fear that I'm not smart enough, that my mind is far inferior to my body and will never accomplish anything on its own. I fear that I don't know how life works off of the field, and that my purpose will be unsettled and ill defined. For the past fifteen years, I've had an itinerary slipped under my door, telling me exactly where I need to be and what I need to do; Sarah always jokes that I'd prefer such an arrangement even when I'm home.

My agent assures me not to worry; I'll be fine. I'll be better than fine. He says believe it or not, Abby, you have more to offer the world than just soccer. People like you. Kids look up to you. Women want to be your friend. Men want to drink whiskey and play golf with you. You have valid ideas about politics, about inequality in sports, about advocating for women. You're funny and articulate and can convince anyone of anything. You could sell a ketchup Popsicle to a woman in white gloves. You will know what you're meant to do when that time comes, but for now, just enjoy where you are.

I decide to take that advice.

On a whim, Sarah and I search online for a home in Portland—friends in the city have been urging us to move—and the perfect one appears on my screen, as if by magic, as if our wishing coaxed it into existence. We send those friends and a realtor to check it out: "Amazing views and great bones," is the consensus; with a gut renovation, it could look exactly like the picture in our minds. On their recommendation alone, I buy it and appoint myself the general contractor. I want to create something out of nothing, a something that will become everything.

I fly out to see the house, the place where I'll have a fresh start. It's perched in the hills outside the city, a perfect balance of bustle and peace. It's made of glossy, warm wood cut in rectangular shapes, the rooms and levels stacked at angles, a structure that reminds me of building blocks. The rear of the first floor features a trio of sliding doors leading out to separate balconies. A stone patio runs the length of the property and looks out onto miles of trees. I begin making it ours, picking out furniture and lighting and finishes. I install a wine refrigerator/beverage center into the kitchen hallway cabinetry, so I don't have to walk to the kitchen for a drink. I visualize the nooks and crannies where our kids will play.

We want three, maybe. Definitely two, at least. Sarah will get pregnant first, after she retires; I will get pregnant next, after I retire. If things are going well, we'll adopt a third, although they always say the third baby is the divorce baby, and we don't ever want to let that happen.

My excitement for a baby surges in August, when Kara gives birth to a boy, Lewis. As soon as I hear the news, I rush to my computer and compose an e-mail:

> Kara,
>
> I'm overcome with excitement. I know we've known each other for many years, but tonight really feels so different. You chose to make a baby, and now he's real. Feel that. You made a stand for what you wanted, and now you have this little one who you will love and nurture for all the days of your life. I am more proud of you now than ever. Feel every moment. You chose a birth plan that not many would choose. You took a chance at doing it organic and natural. I am so proud of you for that. You made a plan and then saw it through. Do you know how cool that is? And to do it vaginally, and in the water. I just have the utmost respect for the way you chose life,—because it is a choice. And you and I get that.
>
> More than anything, I think you are a lover and a survivor, in all that you do. I had no doubts. Today was a certainty for you. I trust you completely and feel you will be a person in my life I can always turn to. Now I have this to be able to ask you questions about. So cool.
>
> Thank you for being in my life, and giving me the gift of

what real love is. It's rare, and a special quality we both have. Just know that today, more than any other, I am sad beyond measure to not be right there by your side. I know you are capable and handled it perfectly, but to be far and not near is surreal and difficult. What makes it easier is to know that you are strong and will be the best goddamn mom in the land. Thank you for the pictures and texts. It meant a lot. Know that I will be doing the same on our blessed day.

We love you beyond imagination. All of you. You, Jenny, Lewis. Can you fucking believe it? You made a human being, Kara. You. Celebrate that. I think you will look back on this as a time of your life that will always uplift you.

In all sincerity, you are my idol, and I love you.

Now rest,

Abby

While I build our home, supervising every last detail, Sarah plans our wedding. It will be grand but intimate, a low-key ceremony involving our closest family and friends. She decides on Hawaii, and I agree, because why not? We want a destination wedding, a place where people would actually want to go on vacation, a place that will make it worthwhile for my siblings to leave their kids behind for a week. She picks a stunning resort called The Villas at Poipu Kai, on Kauai, envisioning a beach ceremony at sunset: her in a flowing white dress, me in a crisp white suit, wearing matching leis.

We pick a date: October 5, 2013. I ask Are to be my best

man, and Dena to read a poem. I'm thrilled Kara can come, even though baby Lewis will only be two months old. Teammates Sydney Leroux and Alex Morgan will be there. Dan Borislow generously offers to pay the bill for the open bar. Our dogs, Tex and Kingston, will be staying behind, but we buy them tuxedos to commemorate the occasion. We file the proper paperwork for a civil union, since same-sex marriage is not yet legal in Hawaii. On the advice of some friends, we go to premarital counseling—just to get our ducks in a row, solidify our respective roles, devise a blueprint for our life.

I am ready. We're ready. I want to be as successful at love as I've been at soccer. It is more important to me than the FIFA award, the Olympic medal, and the World Cup title I have yet to win. On the night before the wedding, after the rehearsal dinner, Sarah and I seclude ourselves in our suite and write our wedding vows.

I am nervous, more nervous than I've ever been—not because of my impending nuptials, but because my mother will be there to witness them. It's all well and good for her to give her blessing to Sarah in private, but this is public, laid out for the world to see. What will she think when I kiss Sarah after our vows? When we have our first dance? Is she going to stand there wishing I had married Are instead? I confide my fears to Dena, and she assures me that my mother has come a long way—even farther than I've hoped. Once, Dena says, when the three of them were in Orlando watching me play,

Are turned to my mother and said, "Your daughter is unfucking-believable." And without batting an eye, my mother replied, "I know, she really is."

I laugh. I've run out of time to be nervous. The procession is going to start soon. I ask Are for the rings and am horrified by his response: he didn't know he was supposed to handle the rings. My cousin Tracy approaches with them, saving the day. As Sarah walks down the aisle my heart bangs against my ribs. A rainbow appears in the sky, arching behind her, and I take it as a good omen.

It's immediately followed by a bad one: We realize that we've left our written vows back in the suite and have to invent new ones on the spot. Still, I've never heard such a lovely string of words—I can barely believe they're intended for me—and I repeat them on the flight home, hoping they'll always be true.

17

GAMBLER

One month after our wedding, standing in the kitchen of our Portland home, Sarah makes an announcement: she will not play another season for the Western New York Flash. She doesn't like Buffalo, as I'm well aware, and wants to focus on creating experiences in our new city. Instead, she'll accept an offer to be traded to the local club team, the Portland Thorns.

Looking across the table at her, our dogs running figure eights through our legs, I contemplate what to say. Later, after having time—too much time—to replay the scene, I'll admit some hard truths about myself: I know I'm a bit of a nightmare to live with, with my need for control constantly at odds with my instinct to go with the flow, my yang stomping on my yin, Intense Abby and Chill Abby in a perpetual showdown, and I'll wonder if Sarah's problem was me as much as it was upstate New York. But in that moment, without benefit of retrospection, I pile all the blame on her. *I've been here before,* I think to myself, when Haley admitted her engagement to a man, and now the fault line from that betrayal cracks further and deepens.

I want to say, "We're newlyweds. We're a family now. If the tables were turned, I'd move to Alaska with you. I just want to be with you, wherever you are. I want you to know you're the most important thing in my life now—more important than soccer."

Instead I say, "Okay, I hear you. I will agree to this decision, but only under one condition: if we start to go south, you have to come to New York, because I make the most money. That's the most logical step. If you haven't gotten a job and we are doing poorly, then everything needs to stop and we need to reconnect."

We kiss, sealing the deal, and in the spring I move back to Buffalo, alone.

From the start, I am miserable without her, and I don't know how to connect to someone when they're not in the room with me. Texting feels superficial, the phone feels like a job, and Skyping is a poor facsimile of the real thing. I seek advice from friends who have been in long-term, long-distance relationships, and their responses are vague: "Yeah, we don't necessarily talk every day. We talk every couple of days. We might text each other to say good morning and good night, but that's mostly it."

That proposed routine is not nearly enough to address my insatiable need for attention, and I begin to flounder and flail, which, as always, leads to drinking. I buy half-gallon bottles of vodka, the serious kind with a briefcase handle. I'll devour half the bottle in one sitting, forcing myself to ration the rest for the following day, and augment my buzz with pills: caffeine tablets, Vicodin, Ambien, security blankets that turn my brain into a warm and vacant place.

I abstain only if the next day features a practice or a game or a tournament with the national team, such as the Algarve Cup, held annually in Portugal. That March, we have our worst showing in history, losing every game in the group stage and finishing in seventh place. I score only twice during the whole tournament and miss a penalty kick, a shot I've made effortlessly dozens of times. In each game, I notice that I shut down in the second half—not just physically but mentally, as though a part of me is back with Sarah in Portland, and I realize I will never play at full capacity again.

My deterioration does not go unnoticed on soccer chat boards, whose members dissect our performance at the Algarve Cup with disgust. "Not only did Abby miss a penalty kick (which makes her PK conversion rate about 50% since 2013)," says one armchair analyst, "but her current fitness level let her squander a prime and easy tap-in for a goal. . . . I recognize her importance on the field, but when does Abby impede the future success of the USWNT?" The next commenter agrees, and adds, "I still think she's very much the heart of the team, but I think she needs to be the heart of the team from the bench. She spends more time flopping around looking for a call than she does playing soccer these days."

I have to admit it's true. If only I were half as talented at flopping around as I once was at playing soccer.

After the tournament, back in Buffalo, I pick up my phone to call Sarah. I hate the dial tone, the ringing, the remote, tinny sound of her voice, three thousand miles away.

"I'm waving the white flag," I say. "You need to come here."

She says no, and explains: She's happy there. She has a life there. I'm so unhappy, and if she moves to Buffalo, the only thing that's going to happen is that she'll be unhappy with me, and that won't be healthy for either of us.

This is not what a relationship should be like, I think. *This is not what our relationship* was *like.* All of our interactions seem tainted by doubt and suspicion. I worry that she has feelings for someone else. Then I worry I'm being ridiculous, creating problems instead of addressing our real ones. But I say nothing. I want her to think everything is still okay—I want everything to *be* okay—and if I don't voice my concerns they might cease to exist, creep back into some far-flung fold of my brain.

When we hang up, I pour myself another glass of vodka.

I deteriorate further in June, during a Western New York Flash game against the last-place Houston Dash, at Sahlen's Stadium in Rochester. In the seventeenth minute, I find the ball and pull back to take a shot. A Houston defender slithers her leg near mine and tries to block it, and as I follow through my foot strikes the ball strangely, sending reverberations up my shin that converge in my knee. *Damn, that hurt,* I think, and feel myself folding to the ground. I'm down a minute, and tell myself it's going to be okay, even though I know I've hurt my knee, and once you've hurt your knee you are never the same. I get up, hobble around, decide I can play, hobble around for another minute and admit that I can't. In the twenty-fourth minute I slump down on the bench, waiting for the trainers to examine me.

"Check and make sure my ACL is there," I plead, and they knead their fingers around my knee and conclude that it is. I'm relieved, and schedule an MRI the following day for an official diagnosis: a sprain of the lateral collateral ligament, which connects the thighbone to the shinbone, and which will take several months to heal.

I decide to view the injury as an opportunity: I'm going back to Portland. *My life is blowing up right now,* I think, *and I need to salvage what I can.*

I am so excited to be home, to feel the dogs lick my face and smell their terrible breath, to see Sarah in the house I built for us. She is sweet and attentive, ordering me to rest, and despite her continuing refusal to come to New York, I want to believe we'll be okay. We meet friends for dinner and I have a glass of wine, and then another, until the glasses amount to a bottle, and when we get home she says words I deserve to hear: "Your drinking is killing us. When you drink, it feels like you're leaving me, like you don't want to be with me, like you want to be by yourself."

"No," I insist. "It's not that. I just don't trust this, what's going on."

Once again I wish I'd voiced my thoughts: *I want to be with you more than anything, but I am afraid of being rejected, of once again feeling unloved and unlovable. If I numb myself enough I won't feel it when the inevitable finally occurs.*

Two more incidents that summer solidify it as the worst of my life. On June 28, a Saturday night, I'm driving along Skyline Boulevard, a narrow, twisty road that winds south of downtown Portland. I take a corner too fast and my Range Rover is airborne, spinning, landing on the roof and collapsing into itself, mimicking my falls on the field. Shards of windshield glass hang like stalactites. When everything goes silent and still, I'm almost afraid to move; I'm not in any pain, but surely I've broken a limb, or sliced my head open, or pulverized my organs so I'm bleeding inside. I unbuckle my seat belt, inch my hand toward the door, fold my body, and slide out. The shards fall; I was a second away from being impaled.

One by one I test my arms and legs and find all my bones intact. A quick rub of my scalp imparts no blood on my hands. Miraculously, I'm unscathed, and I look up and down the road, thankful no one else had been in my path.

Three weeks later, I get a strange message from a teammate about Dan Borislow, my friend and old team owner. She says someone—she doesn't recognize the number—texted her claiming that Dan died of a heart attack, and this person is trying to get in touch with me. I refuse to believe it, and then my phone rings, flashing my mother's name. I almost don't pick up, as if refusing to hear the news will somehow make it untrue.

I relent and answer on the final ring.

"Is he dead?" I ask, without preamble.

"You know?" she says.

By morning, I'm in Florida with his family. Dan was fifty-two, and died after playing a soccer game. He played every bit as hard as he worked—one of the reasons we connected—and while his death is sudden, it's not shocking. I speak at his service in front of five hundred people. "We love you, Dan," I say, and turn to his family. "I'm here for you all." I remember the last time I saw Dan, at my wedding. The morning after the ceremony we held an impromptu poker party on the balcony—alcohol flowing, chips piled up, high rollers only.

In his honor I book a trip to Las Vegas, withdrawing fifteen thousand dollars of the money Sarah and I received for our wedding. I hit table after table, playing poker, blackjack, craps—intending to lose every cent. In fact, I *want* to lose it, and I bet as irresponsibly as I can, hitting on seventeen, placing sucker bets on big six and big eight, making comically bad bluffs. To my frustration, I keep winning, racking up chips hour after hour until I find myself with thirty thousand dollars, double what I came with. *Fuck,* I think. *That's the opposite of what I wanted to happen*. But beneath my dismay I feel a spark of hope: Maybe this is a sign. Maybe we are not yet too far gone. Maybe *I* am not yet too far gone.

18

CHAMPION

In the spring of 2015 I announce that I won't be playing for the Western New York Flash in the upcoming season of the National Women's Soccer League. I release a statement, explaining that I need to prepare mentally and physically for the World Cup tournament, to be held in Canada in June. I'm prepared for the criticism—why am I exempt, when my national teammates have to honor their club commitments?—but not willing to reveal the truth: my sabbatical has nothing to do with the World Cup and everything to do with my troubled marriage.

Sarah herself is doing well, having retired from soccer and secured a job with Nike, carving an identity outside of the sport and cultivating a new group of friends. She had always been dependent on me, and I'm not used to her having a life so removed from the one we'd started together. I hate myself for missing her neediness, for being so needy myself. I had come home in the hope of closing the distance, but my presence seems to make it worse, deepening it by the day. I am the problem no one wants to mention, the elephant in every room.

She proposes a truce, suggesting we should table all our issues until after the World Cup. It's my last chance, and she doesn't want our issues to divert my focus. If I don't win I am going to be angry and disappointed and tormented for the rest of my life. She wants this for me, for us, and she promises to be there for me while I'm on the road. I agree, but I know soccer will never again have all of my mind or heart.

In the midst of these private negotiations, my public life is also getting complicated. FIFA has announced that the women, and only the women, will play their World Cup on artificial turf. In the entire eighty-five-year history of the World Cup, which has seen twenty tournaments for men and six for women, the games have never been played on anything but natural grass. Resources are not an issue—FIFA is worth billions—and it's clear that their decision is rooted in sexism.

Forget our mounting successes and our increasing popularity. Forget the fact that artificial turf negatively impacts our play, changing the way the ball bounces and rolls. Forget that it also increases the risk of injuries, jostling our joints and sloughing off a layer of skin each time we slide against it. Forget that taking a diving header on turf is akin to taking a plunge onto concrete. It's just one more indication that women's soccer is inferior, that women themselves are inferior, and I decide it's time to speak out.

My teammates are equally outraged. Sydney posts a picture on Instagram of her battered and bloodied shins with the caption, "This is why soccer should be played on grass!" Pinoe asserts, simply, that forcing women to play on turf is "bullshit." Celebrities take notice. Los Angeles Lakers star Kobe Bryant shares Sydney's photo, using the hashtag: #ProtectTheAthlete. Tom Hanks follows up with a tweet of his own: "Opinion: Women's World Cup is the best Soccer of the year. Hey FIFA, they deserve real grass. Put in sod." I decide to spearhead a lawsuit against FIFA and the Canadian Soccer Association, charging them with gender discrimination. Forty female international players—from Canada, Brazil, Spain, Japan, and Germany, among others—join me, and the law firm of Boies, Schiller & Flexner (the same firm that successfully argued in favor of same-sex marriage) offers to represent us pro bono.

"It's about doing the right thing, and I think this is the right thing to do," I say in an interview. "We have to fight this fight for this World Cup and World Cups in the future. We have to make sure FIFA knows this is not okay. And they know it's not okay. If you were to ask all of them, they know that they would never do this for the men."

Artificial turf is only one item on my growing list of grievances against both FIFA and U.S. Soccer. Our coaches are not allowed to hire their preferred staff, a restriction that sets them up to fail. There are disparities in the quality of our training: the men's team travels to top facilities around the country, and their expensive equipment—specialty treadmills and weight machines—is shipped along with them. The promotion for our team is subpar; there is no official Women's World Cup app, and the official FIFA app only features the men's World Cup. Most infuriating is the pay gap: the men's team makes more money if they lose games than we do if we win. If we play twenty exhibition games in a season, we each earn a base salary tied to years of service (the highest amount being $72,000), and a $1,350 bonus for each win—a maximum salary of $99,000. For the same schedule, players for the men's team earn a maximum salary of $263,320, and make a base salary of $100,000 even if they lose every game.

It was difficult for me to identify these inequities when I was in the thick of my career, just thrilled to be getting paid for playing my sport. But with the end looming—along with the realization that I am going to have to find another job—I think about them every time I put on my uniform and go to work. For now, the lawsuit is the extent of what I can do, but I know this battle has only just begun.

At training camp in Los Angeles, six hundred miles from Sarah, our problems embed in my mind, accompanying me onto the field. I am not myself, and everyone knows it, and I conclude that the least I can do is admit it out loud. I ask our current coach, Jill Ellis, if we can speak privately.

"Listen," I tell her, "I'm serious. However you want to use me, then that's the way I want to be used, because I need to feel like you want my services. I'll do whatever you need. Trust that I will be ready for the World Cup. No matter what, I always am."

As soon as I finish talking, the answer comes to me: I'll ensure that my teammates have the confidence that I can no longer summon for myself. Pearcie and I attend meetings with the coaching staff, absorb all Jill's concerns and ideas, distill them into specifics, and convey them to the younger players. It's easier for Jill if the captains field doubts and complaints, if we're the bad cops delivering tough news. Her coaching style is effective—the woman knows how to win games—but noncommittal; she doesn't want to criticize her players too harshly for fear of thwarting their focus. I grew up in a family that did its best to avoid messy emotional conversations, and this is my chance to learn to navigate that terrain.

Every day after practice, I text three players an analysis of their performance, tailoring my comments to their personalities—blunt truth for some, gentle suggestions for others. I visit others in their rooms, look them in the eye, and tell them I've been where they are. I've heard the same criticisms, had the same fears, fretted over things I couldn't control. I remind them that we're all Type A women, perfectionists who are the very best at what we do, but none of us will ever be champions alone.

I pay special attention to players who usually don't leave

the bench. In past years, there's been one set roster, with a rotation of three or four players who would be called in to substitute. But this year Jill is devising a different strategy, intending to play many people in many games in different positions, and they all need to be ready. Listen, I tell them, what if there's a chance you might start? What if someone suffers an injury, or you perform beyond expectation at practice, or Jill determines it's your time? Don't let anyone diminish you—least of all yourself—and don't be comfortable with your current status. Think about it, and imagine yourself being better than you ever thought you could be.

I hope my inspirational patter conceals my own doubts: my own best days on the field are long behind me, and I might not leave the bench myself.

In May, just before the World Cup, we face Ireland in an exhibition match. I've played a full ninety minutes in only four of our last thirty games, and I need to regain my stamina and sharpness. It's working, and I'm feeling at ease on the field, scoring two goals in the first half, the 179th and 180th of my career. In the opening minutes of the second half, I try for another, lunging my head against the ball and instead connecting with the elbow of the Ireland goalkeeper. My nose takes the brunt of it, the impact shifting it out of place and unleashing a torrent of blood. It streams through my fingers as I trot to the sidelines.

"Get me one of those cotton balls, stuff it in my nose, and put me back out there," I tell Jill and the training staff. They oblige, and I keep playing, feeling more alive than I have in months.

During the World Cup opener, against Australia, I am mentally alert but can't translate that feeling to my body. My Achilles tendon throbs, reminding me of that injury every time I move my leg. My attempts at headers are awkward, as if I've forgotten the mechanics of the technique; I'm connecting in the wrong spot, miscalculating the distance to the net. We win regardless, 3–1.

In advance of our second game, against Sweden, I have to learn to play the game from the bench. For the first time since 2003, at the World Cup twelve years ago, I am not on the starting lineup for the women's national team. Throughout the first sixty-seven minutes, I sit and scream and cheer from the sidelines, and in the sixty-eighth I'm called on to substitute for Christen Press. The crowd chants my name, telling me they still want to see me play, that I still belong here. I don't score, but neither does anyone else, and the game ends.

For the next few games, depending on Jill's strategy of rotating the roster, I'm in and out, taking my turn on the field and on the bench. I start against Nigeria and, in the forty-fifth minute, blast the ball in with my foot, scoring the only goal of the game. In the knockout round against Colombia, my foot fails me, hooking a penalty kick wide to the left. I see myself miss—the misses are always visible—and I stare at the net in disbelief, my hands covering my mouth. *I'm not my confident self,* I think, *and someone else needs to score.* Carli and Alex do, thankfully, and we notch another win. I ride the bench against China, but once again Carli—wearing the captain's armband—comes through, breaking a scoreless tie with her head, making it look as easy as I once did.

During the semifinal game against Germany, the top-ranked team in the world, I sit on the bench next to Kelley O'Hara, a twenty-five-year-old wingback playing in her second World Cup. "Stay confident," I tell her. "Don't let Jill steal that from you. What if you're called in, and you let her take your confidence for that moment? That moment will be yours. You will shine." And she does, scoring the second and winning goal against Germany.

After the game, she throws her arms around me and says, "That was all you. I would not have survived this tournament, this game especially, if you didn't believe in me."

I pull away from her so I can look her in the eye.

"No," I say, "that was all *you*. Don't forget you were the one who played. You're the one who put yourself in a position to score."

I'm finished with soccer after this tournament, I think. *My job here is done.*

Well, almost done. Before the final game, where we'll face Japan, I record a seven-minute speech, knowing that will have more of an impact than anything I do on the field.

The Fox Sports studio is darkened, and I sit in the swivel stool, rubbing my hands together and rotating my neck, as if I'm warming up to train.

"I might get emotional," I tell the crew. "I think I want to do this alone. Are you guys cool with that?"

They are, and file out of the studio, leaving the camera running. *The words will come,* I think. *Just start talking—you've never had trouble doing that.*

"Finally I have a room to myself," I say, and take a deep breath to begin:

"Everybody keeps asking me what this journey has been and what it will mean if we can be on that top podium Sunday night. I'm not one to necessarily show my vulnerable side, but the days are ticking, and my clock—as it pertains to being a pro soccer player—is coming to an end. But I have a few things I want to get off my mind, and they're all going to be about my teammates.

"I've had the best life. And it's all in total because of the friendships I've made. I've literally grown up on this team, and the good, the bad, and the ugly—my teammates have helped me through it all. And I know that a lot can be said about this World Cup, and how it could be the culmination of my career. And a lot of people have been talking about how this World Cup has been different for me, and the biggest thing I need to express is my gratitude—to be able to have played for so long, to share the field with extraordinary women."

Tears well up, and I shake my head in an attempt to suppress them.

"I can't believe that I'm even getting emotional on camera," I manage. "It's going to be seen by millions. But the truth is, I wouldn't be here if it weren't for my teammates. I wouldn't have scored the goals that I've scored or reached the successes that I've had without them. And the only way we win and get to that top podium is if we fight, and we fight, and we fight some more. And I know, no matter what the outcome of the game on Sunday, that we will all have done our best. I know that, in the thirty-five years of life I've had—such a wonderful life—I've experienced so many things I never thought possible. We're talking about women's soccer now. That's something I'm really proud of, whether I'm on the bench or on the field.

"Putting the crest on every single time means something to me. What would it mean to win this World Cup? It would mean everything. But we're one game away. It's not just going to be handed to us, we know that. We know that from the last time around. We know Japan is going to give us a strong fight. They will not give up. They will not quit. They showed that four years ago; they showed that throughout this entire tournament. We are going to have to play brilliant.

"I want to thank my family. I want to thank Sarah. And my friends who have probably missed me more than anything. People don't get the sacrifices that we make. People don't understand the things that we have to do in order to follow and pursue these dreams that we have. I'm the luckiest person on the planet, and it's not because of any individual award, or even playing on the grandest stage. It's because I've been able to share it. My philosophy in life is that happiness is meant to be shared. And we all have dreams. And if you're out there and you have a dream, and you want something, and you want something so bad . . ."

And here I start crying again, thinking of both soccer and Sarah.

". . . you've got to risk everything. You've got to risk being completely devastated if you don't achieve it. And when you fall down, you've got to get back up. So that's what this means, that's what this is, that's who we are. This team does not lie down for very long. We have an opportunity to take the world by storm. We have an opportunity to bring back the World Cup, back to the United States. We can do it. I know we can do it. We've just got to go out there for those ninety minutes or those 120 minutes, or whatever that game calls for. We have to bring the fire. I know my teammates are going to do whatever they need to do, because I'm going to do it. Whatever my role is, whatever my job is, whatever I'm asked to do, I'm going to do a little bit extra, because I think that's what's it's going to take.

"It's never easy to say goodbye. You always want to go out on top. You always want there to be that fairy-tale ending. I hope that this is it. Not just for me but for this entire group of women who have showed me the way, who have taught me about myself. Who have made me soul-search and find out more about who I am and who I want to be. That's what makes this so special. It's not about wins and losses or even championships. It's about learning, it's about growing, it's about being you.

"I'm proud to be a member of this national team. I've

been proud since I first got the opportunity to wear this jersey, to represent my country. I hope that people know that nobody's perfect. People make mistakes. But on Sunday, if we make mistakes, I know every single player on the field, every single player on the bench, every fan in the stadium, has our back. That is inspiring. To be a part of it, to be able to look at the stands and see my family. No matter what happens, I'm going to be proud of what we've gotten, and where we've gotten to. I'm a lucky person and . . . I know we can do it. We've just got to believe."

I exhale, feeling the weight of those words, and say them one more time: "We've just got to believe."

I keep my promise and do my job, do what I'm asked to do, which means leading from the bench. This is the last World Cup I'll ever play in—one of my last games, period—and *goddamn* do I want to play, to churn up the field with my cleats and feel my head kiss the ball. Instead I watch my team deliver an exuberant beat-down: one goal at minute three, another at minute five, another at minute thirteen, another at minute fifteen. I almost—*almost*—feel sorry for the Japanese players, wandering around as though the field is some postapocalyptic landscape they've never before seen. Close to halftime it becomes more familiar, and they find their way to the goal, slipping one into our net. My mind conjures the memory of my lost high school championship, the last time I lusted this fervently for a win. For five minutes straight I scream expletive-laden advice, sending teammates scuttling away from me. Sydney bravely turns to me and gives a stern order: "Okay, enough." I promise to try. After the break Japan scores again—prompting more screams and expletives and scampering teammates—but we answer in the very next minute, and now it's 5–2.

They're getting desperate, tossing themselves at the ball, and goddamn do I still want to play; I was always the reliable and foolproof closer, and I need to be on the field as the clock winds down, even if there's nothing to close. I cry as I warm up, knowing that my team is giving me a gift, and instruct myself to pull it together before I step on the field. In the seventy-ninth minute Jill sends me in to replace Tobin Heath. When I reach the line, Carli meets me there. She removes the captain's armband and wraps it around my bicep, a gesture I didn't expect but appreciate immensely, a reverse passing of the torch.

The field, even covered in the dreaded Astroturf, has never felt so sweet beneath my feet. Right away I'm off, galloping like a thoroughbred, relishing the chase and the capture; an opponent tackles me and earns a yellow card. In the eighty-sixth minute, Pearcie comes on. She's forty years old, the last veteran standing from the 99ers, and this is also her last World Cup. Four minutes later the whistle blows and the celebration begins; I fall to my knees and raise my face to the sky. When I pull myself up I see my teammates, collected in a tight huddle and pulsing like a heart.

But my eyes sweep to the left and zero in on Sarah, who's

wearing a jersey decorated with my name. I lumber toward her, tentatively at first, and then pick up speed. My arms lift up and she leans down, meeting me halfway, draping herself like an ornament over the railing. I loop my arm around her back, using it as scaffolding; I am worried she's going to fall. She wraps her hands around my face, fingertips meeting at the back of my neck, and looks me in the eye.

"I did it," I whisper. "*We* did it."

"Kiss me," she commands.

In the moment, I am not thinking about politics, or the fact that gay marriage was legalized by the Supreme Court a week earlier. It doesn't occur to me that a video of our kiss will go viral, or that I will be asked to articulate what was running through my mind. Publicly, I'll say, "In that moment as a human being, you ask yourself—who's the one person I want to run to, the person who sacrificed with me and dried my tears and wiped my blood and listened to my issues?" Privately, I'm thinking, *Even after what what've been through, she's still capable of being there for me. We've set aside all our issues for this, and now it's here, and we won, and it's in the past, and now we can work on finding our way back to each other.*

And so I obey, kissing her like no one is watching at all.

19

ADVOCATE

Despite all the attention, the viral video, the headlines declaring that we exemplify "what love looks like," the high from that kiss doesn't last. The issues that plagued us before the World Cup only worsen after it's over. My marriage becomes my new obsession, the sole receptacle of my focus, and it buckles under the weight of my neediness. Every word is misinterpreted, every glance tinged with anger or regret. I want what we once had. I chase it, I scour corners for it. It's not anywhere, and I choose to get lost along with it.

The various pills I took to do my job, I now needed to live my life. I trade the caffeine pills for straight-up Adderall, popping one in the morning, along with coffee. I trade the Vicodin for Norco, which has a higher concentration of opioids, popping one or two as soon as the Adderall buzz wears off. I keep my old bedtime standby, Ambien, but increase the amount of alcohol I drink to help it along. I wonder how I'll cope when I no longer have access to my prescriptions. I wake up, painfully aware of my feelings, and start the process of killing them all over again.

It's a relief when I have to go on the road for the team's victory tour, although initially I had protested the idea. I didn't want the fanfare of a long goodbye, the spotlight in each stadium fixing relentlessly on me. My teammate Shannon Boxx urges me to reconsider, insisting that I owe it to all my teammates and all my fans, that I should think of it as a celebration not just of my career but of all the progress women's soccer has made. It's bigger than just me. I can't argue with that. Besides, I reason, maybe the distance will help my domestic situation this time around. Maybe the act of playing and giving interviews will dislodge my negative thoughts.

It does, intermittently. I'm secretly thrilled when fans gather at the airport to meet our arriving plane. I joke with reporters that I'll have to revert back to my natural hair color because my current platinum hue makes me instantly recognizable. We're not allowed to sign autographs in hotels, but I always stop to talk to kids, shaking their hands and telling them to be brave. I wade back into the gender equality issue, declaring that I'll keep fighting even though we dropped our turf lawsuit. (Our lawyers realized that FIFA was going to slow-play the case, rendering a decision *after* the World Cup, thereby weakening our fight.) I announce that soccer is the next big thing in the United States, and corporations would be smart to get in on the ground floor.

"Get on it, people," I urge. "You guys are going to miss out if you don't. . . . It's an amazing time not only to be a footballer here in the U.S., but to be a female soccer player. We know that bringing home championships just gives us a better platform and another opportunity to start a conversation to get a little bit more pay, and bring that gap closer together."

Every good day is chased by a bad one. I continue with my pill cocktail and my press junkets. I text with Sarah: "Are we losing something that was once beautiful? Can we ever re-create happiness again?" Neither of us has answers. My roommate on the road, Sydney, tries to go to sleep before I do to escape my dreadful snoring. As insurance, she wears headphones or earplugs. Some nights I see her watching me, my fingers doing their familiar lap from the bottle to my mouth. Once, she kicks off her covers, pulls out her phone, and retrieves one of her favorite poems. She reads it to me softly in the dark:

there will always be
parts of me that only you
can unlock,
that only you can come back to save

and that only you can calm, too soon.
what remains of me,
will always fill
the emptiness in you.
it will always complete all that we have.
the only parts
we have not learned
to say goodbye to.
the only parts where we
can still be free.

I know it's her way of saying she is worried about me.

On October 27, a Tuesday, the national team visits the White House and meets President Barack Obama. The whole event is surreal to me, on multiple levels: here's a butch lesbian meeting our first black president—a president who deems female athletes worth celebrating on the most visible stage in the world. "They've inspired millions of girls to dream bigger and, by the way, inspired millions of boys to look at girls differently, which is just as important," Obama says. "This team taught all America's children that playing like a girl means you're a badass."

We'd been warned beforehand not to request selfies, but the president slyly undermines this edict. Turning to the crowd, he quips, "I'm sure you'd all love to take selfies with them." I decide to go for it. "Mr. President," I say, "how about you taking a selfie with us, then?"

I hold out my phone and capture everyone's face but my own; only a streak of my platinum hair appears along the edge. The best unselfie ever snapped.

As soon as we leave the White House, I announce my retirement from soccer, ending my written statement with the words, "I can't wait to see what the next chapter of my life brings." I take phone calls from the press, doing my best to redirect the focus back to the team. "It's time for me to walk away," I tell *USA Today*. "I know the young studs—the Sydney Lerouxs, the Alex Morgans—they're the ones that will take this game to the next paradigm and that's something I'm excited to watch and see grow. Thinking about my teammates and time spent with them, that's what I'm going to miss most. It's not going to be the sprints, it's not going to be the traveling, it's not going to be—even in some small way—the game. It's going to be the people that I've been literally able to grow up with."

That night, alone in my room at the W Hotel, I craft a rare prepared speech to give at tomorrow's luncheon with the National Press Club. I labor over it, organizing my thoughts and fretting over the words; I want it to sound like the best version of myself.

"Character is a funny thing," I write somewhere in the middle. "I've found that your character is tested the most when things don't go your way."

Things will be going my way soon, I tell myself. *They have to.*

The team's victory tour is suspended in November, to be concluded the following month, but I don't go home. Instead I travel to San Antonio, Gainesville, New York City, Boston, Washington, D.C., Chicago, Milwaukee, Nashville, and Houston. I speak at fundraisers and attend galas and shoot commercials, including one for Gatorade in which I implore everyone to forget me (*but only with regard to soccer,* I think, *not for good!*). I partner with Triax Technologies to promote their head impact monitor and talk about concussion awareness and safety. I recall how I foolishly stayed on the field after I'd suffered one myself, back in 2013. My teammate, standing a few yards away, kicked a line-drive shot straight at my head, the impact felling me like a chopped tree. An opposing player approached and asked if I was all right; I mumbled my answer, my mouth incapable of forming proper words.

"I've headed the ball so many times throughout my career, so does it gives me pause thinking what my future looks like?" I ask Fox News. "Of course it does, so I want to put athletes in control of their lives so they don't have that kind of pause."

I speak at children's soccer fundraisers, where I peer out at all those sweet, earnest faces and worry about lying to them. At one event, a ten-year-old girl waits her turn in line at my autograph table. I do a double take; she's wearing my exact hairstyle, buzzed on the sides and longer on the top.

She is me twenty-five years ago, had I been brave enough then to defy my mother and cut my ponytail.

"Hey, your hair is so cute," I tell her. "Can I take a photo of you for some ideas for my next cut?"

She complies, squeezing in next to me.

After the click, I bring the girl around to the other side of the table, where no one can hear us, and tell her I have a question: "Does anyone think you look like a boy?"

Before she can answer, I speak again. "It happens to me all the time and it's not something to worry about. See, you and me, we aren't that different at all."

She nods, her mouth set in a serious line, and I know she understands.

In Seattle, after an event, I call Haley and ask if I can see her. She lives in that city now with her husband and two children, and has a job as a social worker at an elementary school. We meet at her school and take a walk around the neighborhood, and for once our conversation seems stilted and restrained. Later, she'll tell me she knew something was wrong: I looked unhealthy, pallid, thin. I wasn't the Abby she'd known for years, raw and real. Instead I was "Business Abby," distant and remote, using the voice I reserve for speaking to the press. She asks me how I'm feeling about my impending retirement, and I reach for the phrases I've crafted and polished. It's so exciting, and so many opportunities are falling into my path, and I'm going to be able to make a real difference and have a positive impact on people's lives. She nods and says she's so happy for me, and at those words I let my mask fall.

"There's one thing," I say, and attempt a light laugh. "I'm going to have to drink a little bit less."

Half the time I am a chatty wind-up toy that keeps churning its own crank, the other half an extinguished fire that will never reignite. My weight soars and plummets, plummets and soars, my body expanding and erasing itself as fast as it can. The needle in my mind oscillates along with it. I am bulging with confidence and swagger and excitement; I am despondent and convinced everything is futile in the end. When I'm on the upswing, my ideas beget ideas and I connect with people who can help me make them real.

"I am going to change the world," I write to one, "and you will join me. Lots and lots of stuff happening to create a platform, property, conversation, equal opportunity . . . Basically create an empire where the sole focus is to make it a societal norm for men and women to be equals. Not just in sports either. And not just in this country. I want it all. I want it global. The time is now . . . and I'm going to create something to finally get the job done. I am still ironing out a map as to how it will all happen, and I want to form a coalition of other like-minded badass women to figure out a way to ensure equal opportunity for all human beings (minus Donald Trump) happens.

"Okay . . . I could go on, but like I said, it would not do it justice. And to be up front, this all has just hit me like a ton of bricks since announcing my retirement. Basically I'm fucking pissed off I have to find work after my career because I'm a woman. And I'm done with being angry and turning it on its head and just going all in to change it. Now is the time. And I am in a unique position to actually help do it.

"Not to be arrogant or overly confident but there is something symbolic about saying you 'will' do something, rather than you 'want' to. And since saying I will change the world, doors that you can't imagine have just swung open and I'm going for it.

"Please let's chat soon!!! I'm fired up. So much work to do, but man isn't this gonna be fun."

I have an emotional déjà vu: this is how I felt when I first realized I was good at soccer—not just good, but one of the best in the world, doing what I was surely born to do. I can be just as successful at advocacy. "I know I am sounding crazy in every way," I confide to my agent. "But this is how I am processing through this. I am righteous right now. Please know I won't lose myself in this, but that in fact I'm finding myself and the voice I want to convey. I am in the brainstorming stage. Some shit I say and feel is batshit crazy for now. I get that. I just need to say it and get it out there. Passion is a fickle thing. It's not always right or possible. But someone has to have the courage to say what others won't say aloud. . . . We need a plan. I feel like the *Jerry Maguire* movie."

The idea lodges inside my mind and begins to take shape.

I picture an umbrella organization whose sole goal is pursuing equal pay and working conditions. I'll connect with leaders in media and politics so there's a point person working to effect change across the board, starting from the grassroots level and eventually lobbying for legislation in Washington. We'll build and grow these platforms, assisting each other's efforts and sharing results. It'll be the female equivalent of the old boys' club, an organization that will grow and flourish with each successive generation. We'll reach underserved and underprivileged kids, teaching them leadership skills and inspiring them to imagine a world beyond the one they already know.

I'll be in charge of the sports sector, working with each individual team to ensure compliance. I'll point out the absurdity in soccer's pay gap: My team split $2 million in prize money after winning the World Cup, whereas the victorious German men's team received $35 million last summer. I'll argue that FIFA should spend more money promoting women's soccer ($73 million on our World Cup, compared to $2.2 billion for the men) and be more transparent with its finances; currently they offer no concrete figures about how much revenue we generate.

U.S. Soccer's monetary figures are equally unsettling. In 2017, the women's team is expected to generate $17 million in revenue compared to $9 million by the men, and yet the men's salaries still dwarf the women's across the board. For wins, the women's team earns thirty-seven cents to every dollar earned by men. Players in the National Women's Soccer

League earn between $6,842 and $37,800, while members of Major League Soccer earn an average salary exceeding $200,000. The growing popularity of women's soccer will help me make my case. Our World Cup final against Japan attracted 750 million viewers worldwide and was the most watched soccer match in U.S. history; our viewership even trumped the 2015 NBA championship featuring Stephen Curry and LeBron James. Even if it's too late to benefit from my own advocacy, I want future generations to be granted the respect and compensation they deserve.

I'll work as hard at striving for equality as I did perfecting headers. I'm stubborn, strong-willed, tenacious. I am fiercely devoted to the concept of fairness. I have always followed my own path, seeking authenticity even before that became a trendy word, and I can inspire others to do the same. I don't quit. I *won't* quit, no matter what happens.

Except for soccer. I have to quit soccer.

Before I do, I have one last month of games for the national team's victory tour. In December, we're scheduled for four matches across the country, beginning in Honolulu and ending on December 16 in New Orleans. I spend the entire flight to Hawaii researching Teslas, and as soon as we land I order one online. My new car is the highlight of that trip; we decide we should cancel our match in Aloha Stadium, since their artificial field looks like it hasn't been replaced in years.

Instead we play Trinidad and Tobago in San Antonio, a 6–0 win, and then beat China in Glendale, Arizona, my penultimate game. Before the whistle blows, instead of taking charge of the huddle and unleashing my usual medley of encouragement and obscenities, I hold back and say nothing. To my delight, two of my teammates step forward and run the huddle, and I know I am leaving the team—and the game—better than I found it.

After we celebrate and I drink my vodka and take my pills, I lie on my bed, trying to freeze my mind, to keep my concerns and fears and hopes quiet for just a few hours, long enough to sleep before they start all over again. My mind ignores my request, and all night I think of the end of soccer and the beginning of something else, still wonderfully mysterious and exciting. I think of Sarah, who plans to come to my last game even though we're barely speaking, even though we have no idea what we are. *Retirement is not peaches and cream,* I think, *and I'll talk about that when the time comes. People don't talk about the hard transitions enough, the hard bits of life. Strength is a full gamut. You've got to be strong from top to bottom, but you also have to raise your hand and say, "I'm feeling weak right now. I need some help." There is true strength in being able to ask for help.*

Without meaning to, I start to cry, tears hitting my pillow like a clichéd love song, and at least I'm strong enough to let them fall. Poor Sydney, trying to sleep across the room, hears me through her earplugs. From the corner of my eye I see her sit up and remove them, and then take careful steps to my bed. She lies down and makes room for herself, crying right along with me.

20

CONTROL FREAK

One of the like-minded, badass women I've been speaking to offers a metaphor that perfectly captures this moment in my life. We're talking about retirement and transitions, the challenges involved in letting go of the only work and life you've ever known. Trapeze artists are so amazing in so many ways, she says, because they are grounded to one rung for a long time, and in order to get to the other rung they have to let go. What makes them so brilliant and beautiful and courageous and strong is that they execute flips in the middle. The middle is their magic. And if you're brave enough to let go of that first rung, she concludes, you can create your own magic in the middle.

I think about that magic, *my* magic, as I compose an e-mail to my inner circle before the final game:

Hey guys,

First off, I just want to thank all of you for taking the time to come to my last game. Gosh, even as I type that, I feel relief (while drinking a glass of red wine). It's time and I have known for a while.

Anyways, I (with a nudge from a friend) just wanted to write to you guys telling you all "why" I want all my closest friends and family there with me. And I will totally mess up how I would say it to your faces, so bear with me—I'm a much better talker than writer.

I don't want you guys to feel bad for one moment about the way these few days will go (me being excessive with flights, hotels, etc.). It's gonna be crazy fun, and I wanted to create an environment to in some way SHOW you all how I feel about you and the support you've given me during my time as your friend. You see, I only have—and AM—everything because of the support system that I've been lucky enough to be around.

I know you guys see the "Fun Abby," out at bars and going on vacation more often than not, but for the most part of my life I've been gone, alone, in search of something . . . I think that's why I fell so hard for every one of you. It's because you can see me searching for something, and love the parts of me that don't always equate to this "pro" athlete, yet you still never judged my character. I can't tell you how valuable THIS kind of personal acceptance you all have given me, during my time as a soccer player, has been.

What I *do* know is that your acceptance HAS defined me!! You all, not the game, have helped me find myself a place in this world. And it's so bizarre to be writing this and have no idea where my next paycheck will come from . . . I just want you all there for me, in my last moments identifying as a soccer player, to remind me of who I am, and who I want to be, and that soccer isn't ALL of who I am. It was a part of the search . . . Here's the thing . . . what I have found is that I will always be in search. It's who I am.

Cheers to closing this chapter in my life, and I can't wait to see what goes on and happens on our next pages together. I wouldn't want to spend time between these trapeze bar rungs with any other people. People need to hold on and feel safe and secure, and I've had soccer my entire life to secure me and make me confident and make me think I knew who I was. . . . These last few years have been a struggle for me in soccer. And so finally, I'm letting go of the trapeze rung and letting some MAGIC happen in the middle.

Before I grab on to the other side, I need some magic (crazy, or danger, or risk, or love, or to let myself become un-fucking-raveled) and I know, with all you beauties by my side, I will be just fine. I may cry—that's okay, I'm in touch with that part of myself. I may drink too much—tell me, "Don't be a stupid idiot, you don't run around now for a living, dumbass." But what I need you all to know is that sometimes being in search of something greater doesn't mean it's always out there. Sometimes I may need someone (Sarah) to pull me back home to planet Earth.

Quite frankly, I don't know what tomorrow brings, and that freedom for the first time, and truly accepting it, is something new, and something I'm growing fond of minute by minute. My confidence is coming back. I'm regaining that "it" factor I stopped being able to muster on the field. I'm honest with myself about that, don't worry. What I do know is I can call on any one of you if I ever need anything. And maybe I always overdo it, because I just want you guys to love me (control freak, and fear of being unlovable) and so I give you anything I think would make you all happy and fulfilled. That is my own bullshit I gotta sort through, but this trip is different. It is only a big fucking THANK YOU!! Come, enjoy, and let's see what kind of shit we can do in the magic. I bet it will be glorious and splendid.

I am the lucky one.
Forever grateful,
Abby

The only thing I like less than rules is the complete absence of them—as long as they're ones I craft and enforce myself. Over the course of fifteen years, from my first appearance in a national game to my last, I've developed a pregame ritual that combines the pedantry of Sun Tzu and the paranoia of Howard Hughes. Depending on the quality of my play in any given game, I add and subtract and modify superstitions, certain that a minor tweak to the formula will set things right again. By my 255th international appearance on December 16, the last game of my career, the ritual looks like this:

Two hours before the whistle blows, I eat a plate of chicken and salad, with a side of caffeine pills. The chicken serving must be modest, no larger than the size of my fist, because I want to be light and fast. I drink a gallon of water straight from the jug, hydrating myself nearly to the point of nausea, and then test fate by drinking even more, chugging down a few helpings of Gatorade as pregame fuel. On the way to the game, I usually call Sarah and play solitaire; on this day, I do only the latter. I have to win before I reach the stadium, and the number of attempts it takes is either a good or bad sign. When I get to the locker room I drop my bags off, line up my gear, and remove my jewelry.

First to come off: a family heirloom ring made of diamonds from my grandmother's wedding band, which I wear on my right hand. I slip it off and lay it in the middle of my locker. Only when it's placed safely in its spot can I begin the task of getting dressed and taped. I pull on my sliders—the tight underwear that protects your legs from chafing against turf—and then my shorts and a warm-up T-shirt. I'm ready to be taped, a complicated, painstaking process that can go terribly wrong, requiring multiple do-overs.

One of my trainers tapes my left ankle first, then my right—no reason for the order, but once it worked it became law. I stand up, flex and point each foot, and then head back to the locker room, where my teammates are all immersed in rituals of their own. Sitting on a bench, I pull on my socks (first left, then right), my cleats (left, right), and shin guards (left, right). Now it's back to the training room for more taping, where I have to select exactly the right roll of tape. It must be fairly used but flat to the touch, with no ridges or wrinkles. Sometimes my trainer will forget and hand me the tape. "No, put it down," I say. "I have to pick it up myself." Once I do, I return to the locker room, handling the roll of tape as though it's a fragile artifact.

It gets weirder.

I plop down on the bench again and hold the roll aloft. In between taping parts of my body, and parts of my clothing that need to adhere to my body, I have to rip off a strip, making a clean slate, so that each successive piece of tape has its own specific purpose with no connection to the previous piece. I stick these "clean slate" strips on my knees, to be dealt with at the end.

But first, carefully, I unfurl a long ribbon of tape and cut it roughly in half, so that the pieces are not quite even. I wind the larger piece around the sock for my left shin guard; the smaller piece is always reserved for the right. If I don't cut correctly and the pieces look identical, I have to remove all the tape, fetch a new roll, and restart the entire process from scratch. If I do it correctly, it winds around like a necklace, the two ends connecting seamlessly in the back.

I rip off two "clean slate" strips, place one on each knee, and repeat the process, this time taping above each shin guard (left, right). When those are finished, I press two more clean slate strips along my knees.

It gets weirder still.

The tape also acts as a substitute for my rings, both my grandmother's and my wedding rings, since we're not allowed to wear jewelry when we play. By the end of my career, I'm adept at yanking a piece of tape so that I end up with just the right amount, a width and heft that accurately reflects my level of neediness: a thin strip if I'm feeling confident, a thicker one if I'm not. I wrap one piece around my right ring finger and another on my left, a sign to my wife that she is with me on the field. On this night, for the first time, I leave my fingers bare; Sarah and I are not even in a place where I want her represented by a strip of tape. She'll be at the game, sitting in box seats, and I know she'll notice its absence.

It's time to discard the clean slate strips, which involves an entirely separate ritual. One by one, I rip off the pieces on the left knee and fold them into themselves so that the corners precisely align, creating a triangular wad. I find the trash and release each wad with a flick of the wrist, spinning it like a helicopter into the can. If the wads don't spin properly, or if I miss, I have to attempt all three again.

But by then, the damage is done, and I'm convinced it's not my day. Regardless, the entire process must then be repeated on the right side.

It's not over yet.

In games past, when Rachel Buehler was still on the team, her pregame routine had been a vital part of my own. She sat by her locker and retrieved pictures of people and things she loves. I looked not at her photos but at her face, watching her reactions, riding shotgun on her emotions. Now, without Rachel here, I'll take a peek at Alex Morgan, who, before every game, curls herself into a ball at the bottom of her locker, head clamped between her knees, finding quiet amid the chaos.

When we're ready for warm-ups, I have to be the first one out of the locker room; everyone is aware of and complies with this quirk. Of course, I have to lead with my left foot, and my left foot must touch the field first. Then I back away and step directly on the line, left then right. Now my crazy is sufficiently quelled, and I can begin to move, jogging a few laps before I stretch each leg, left and right.

Then the crazy resurfaces.

I find a ball and juggle it twenty-five times with my feet. On the last one, I pop it up, trying to trap it on its way down. If I succeed, I know I'm going to have a good game (a successful trap might even mitigate the damage done by a poorly aimed wad of tape). I've made it my job to grab the practice jerseys—or "pinnies"—for the pre-game scrimmage, always handing the first one to Pearcie. During drills, I have to score, kicking the ball through the gates. If I miss or hit a cone, the successful juggling no longer matters, and I'm doomed.

Sometimes it helps, especially toward the end of my playing career, to lay blame anywhere but on myself.

We take off our pinnies, throw them down, and move on to our official shooting practice. "Let it ride," I'll say to whomever is covering the goal, and they know not to block the shot. Practice is the only time I can witness the ball hit the net, and I try to carry that image with me for when it will actually count.

I have to be the second one back in the locker room; our goalkeeper, Hope, is always the first. She's engaged in her own pregame ritual, systematically changing her whole outfit, down to her socks.

"Here we go, Hope!" I say.

"Here we go, Abs!" comes the immediate reply.

For as long as I can remember it's been our standard call and response, as automatic as "Amen" after a prayer.

We're almost there.

Everyone lines up to go to the bathroom, and I have to use the middle stall. Pearcie summons us over for our pregame pep talk, reminding us of strategy, of trick plays our opponents might attempt. Everyone trickles out onto the field and I'm the last in line. Our coaches are waiting for us, lined up a row with their hands raised, prepared to give high fives. When I reach them I pull my hand back and snap it forward with every ounce of strength, intent on making these high fives the most solidly executed and painful in high-five history. I approach the field, measuring out my steps so that once again the left taps the grass first.

When the national anthem comes on, I lower my head, close my eyes, and picture myself scoring a header goal. After the words "home of the brave" reverberate and fade, I hop lightly, three times. Back at our bench, someone hands me water. I squirt two shots into my mouth, spit it out, and then spray water all over my hair and shake my head like a freshly bathed dog. With my face still wet, I slap my cheeks three times as hard as I possibly can; the sound and the sting are the last signals to my body, assurance that it's ready.

At long last, there's the huddle on the field—my cursing, my stammering, my leading the "Oosa" chant—and then I find my position, jumping as high as I possibly can and mimicking a header, my eyes connecting with the net while they still can.

It's over, and it's just beginning.

My coach and my teammates insist on starting me, even though I'm ill prepared and unfit, for once underweight instead of over. The crowd, all 32,950 of them, transforms my name into a song—*AB-BY WAM-BACH (clap clap, clap clap clap)! AB-BY WAM-BACH (clap clap, clap clap clap)!*—and the beat lingers in my ears long after they stop. People wave enormous cardboard cutouts of an earlier version of my face, pinker and plumper. I hang in effigy over the railing, a red, white, and blue banner made to resemble Obama's "Hope" poster. Earlier that day the president tweeted about my last game: "Congrats on a great career, Abby Wambach. For the goals you've scored & the kids you've inspired, you're the GOAT!"

The whistle blows, and I do not feel like the GOAT. In fact, before the game, I hadn't even known the meaning of the acronym ("greatest of all time"); I thought the numerous Twitter mentions were insults and accusations, that I had finally been exposed, and my agent had to reassure me that wasn't the case. Now, my teammates take every chance to pass me the ball, but it seems like a live thing, moving of its own accord, rolling out of reach every time I get close. I am sad, listless Rocky, being outrun by chickens before Mickey whips him into shape. By the middle of the first half, I start screaming: "We need a goal! Don't worry about trying to get *me* a goal—*we* need a goal!" They keep passing the ball to me anyway, and my best shot, from twelve yards out, skitters weakly toward China's net. At halftime, in the locker room, my teammates take turns apologizing to me. There's nothing to be sorry about, I tell them. Today is not about getting a result. It's about celebrating our team and the time I've spent with them.

In the seventy-second minute, Jill calls me off, and the sound of applause follows me to the bench. *Symbolic,* I think. *I had seventy minutes and I can't score. It really is time for me to step away.* No one else scores, either—they had spent all their time passing the ball to me—and we lose, 1–0, our first defeat on American soil in 104 games.

Privately, I am devastated beyond measure. I did not want to lose; I have never in my life been comfortable with losing. I wanted it to end, but not like this. I don't want that stumbling, slow-motion performance to be the last recorded footage of my career. I'm also worried about my own postgame celebrations. My family is unaware of my marriage troubles, and I can only imagine the faux cheery conversations Sarah has been having with them, the imaginary narrative she's stitching together. Will she tell them I asked her to skip the after-party? That I was too afraid of us fighting and making a scene and ruining the whole night? At the same time, I am amazed that she's come at all, once again ignoring her own hurt and pain just to support me. *With soccer ending,* I think, *I might finally be able to show up for her. The real me, not the me I am right now.*

Standing in the center of the field, thousands of cardboard doppelgängers waving back at me, I take the microphone and address the crowd. "I'm going to make this short," I say. "I love you guys. I love this team. I love my country. And it has been my pleasure and honor to represent all of you for as long as I've been able to."

Someone in the nosebleed section screams, "Thanks, Abby!" the words so loud and clear it's as if he whispered them face-to-face.

"My family, my friends, you guys in the suites"—I think of Sarah but don't say her name—"I wish I was there right now. But I think symbolically, the way this game went, means this team, for me, I can walk away. The future is so bright. These women are going to kill it. I know it. And before I get all emotional, I just want to genuinely express how much I have given myself to this team, and how important"—I have to pause to stop myself from crying—"and how important it is to give all of yourself to whatever you want to do in your life as a passion."

I turn toward my team. "I love you guys so much," I say. "Bourbon Street, watch out."

I drop the mic on the field with a muted thud.

Wambach, *out*.

21

ADDICT

I never need sleep anymore. I can stay up until six in the morning and be at breakfast by eight. I have much to do, to see, to think about, to plan. Hillary Clinton's people ask me to campaign for her after the holidays. The president of Equinox, Sarah Robb O'Hagan, congratulates me on my "amazing year" and tells me she can't wait to witness the next phase of my life. To that end, might she introduce me to Wharton professor Adam Grant? He's planning the next People Analytics Conference and thinks I'd make an interesting addition to the lineup. I speak with Apple CEO Tim Cook, who agrees that treating people equally and fairly is ultimately good for business. At the Facebook offices in San Francisco, I meet for hours with Sheryl Sandberg in a glass-walled conference room, situated like a giant fishbowl in a hallway maze. "Stick to your guns," she tells me. "Focus on the feminist aspects of inequality, and the rest will work itself out."

On another visit to Facebook, I try the not-yet-released Oculus Rift, a virtual reality device that immerses you in a futuristic, three-dimensional world. The Facebook employee slips the headset over my ears and asks, "Are you creative?" I tell him no, not at all, but as I work the controller and wander through this alternate universe, I reconsider my response. Isn't rebellion a form of creativity? My lifelong search to find alternative routes to be better and faster, to excel at the highest level with minimal effort? Even *this*—my all-consuming, frenetic obsession with changing the world—involves a creative suspension of disbelief: if I direct my energy externally, on forces and factors far away, I won't have time to examine the wreckage all around me. I can control what I envision for others, but my own life plan has been irrevocably derailed.

I briefly go home—not to Portland but to Rochester, where the town throws me a retirement party and I weep multiple times onstage. It's a live, Technicolor episode of *This Is Your Life,* complete with corporate sponsors. Most of the attendees have known me since childhood, teachers and coaches and the local paper's sports journalist, and a part of me longs to regress, to wake up on a day where my biggest problem is falsifying a book report or rebelling against curfew. Mercy's field has been rechristened the "Abby Wambach '98 Field." Current soccer players for Mercy talk about why they admire me. "She holds herself in a way where she's not cocky, but she's very determined and passionate," says one team captain. "She inspires a lot of young women to want to be better," says the other. "It's just amazing."

My sister Laura tells favorite family stories: One Christmas I insisted that everyone do a random act of kindness; mine was to leave money in a copy of *The Giving Tree* at the local Barnes & Noble. I used to lick each French fry so none of my siblings would want to eat them, and I'd have the whole plate to myself. Last summer I held fishing contests for my nieces and nephews at our house in the Thousand Islands, promising hundreds of dollars of Beats by Dre speakers and headphones as the prize. "We don't accept ties," I warned them. "There's only one champion. Get out there and fish—we need a winner." Afterward I apologized to them for being so tough, and explained that I was trying to teach a valuable lesson: life makes people work for what they want.

My nephew Ben thanks me for inspiring him to be a better teammate and person. He will never forget a question I once asked him: "Who do you want to be and how do you want to get there?" My mother imagines all the exciting things I am going to do with the talents the good Lord has given me. The local sports reporter, who has covered my career since high school, calls me a role model and a "guiding light" and says he can't deliver a bigger compliment than this: if his two-year-old daughter grows up to be half the woman I am, he'll be a lucky, lucky father.

I take the stage to deafening applause. "If you dream anything, if you want something, just go after it," I say. "You might surprise yourself."

From Rochester I fly to New York City for business meetings. My agent travels with me, making sure I keep to my schedule, compiling notes and ideas for my "equality manifesto." Before we part ways he takes me aside.

"Are you okay?" he asks. "You need to take care of yourself. You look unhealthy, and I'm worried about you. You have to understand that your greatest quality—your willingness to take risks, and to do and say things that others aren't—is your secret sauce. It's what draws people to you. And if they think that it's fueled by alcohol or drugs, and that it isn't coming from *you*, it's all going to go away. Think about that." I agree, and spend the rest of that trip detoxing on the floor of my hotel room. I sweat my ass off. My skin smells of waxy chemicals. My eyes leak. I can't stop yawning but I can't sleep. I hate the world. I hate myself. Unbeknownst to me, a few concerned friends have begun to hatch a plan; they call it "Operation Get Abby Back."

On December 21, I fly back to Portland, where my brand-new Tesla and another stash of pills are waiting for me.

When I get home, Sarah and I have the worst fight of our marriage to date. I am gripped by the need to remove myself from the situation. If I stay, I know I will pick up my pills again, wash them down with too much vodka, and ruin all the hard work I did in that hotel room. Instead I throw clothes, toiletries, and a few bottles of pills into a suitcase, start up my Tesla, and head south to Los Angeles. I think of the trip I took eleven years ago, back in 2004, when I drove thirty-two hours straight from Florida to Phoenix to see Haley, to hear her admit in person that she had been with someone else. I don't eat, I don't sleep, I stop only to charge the car and to block Sarah's phone number and e-mail. *I need to go in search of happiness,* I think. *There are too many highs and lows, too much back and forth between incredibly awesome shit and moments where I have no idea what I'm doing or who I am. Why is it that when one part of my life ends, every part of my life ends?* When I arrive in Los Angeles, it's twenty hours later, and Kara opens her door to let me in.

When we're alone, out of earshot of her partner and son, I pull out a paper bag crammed with my drugs—bottles of Norco, Adderall, Xanax, Ambien. From my wallet I retrieve my last prescription. Holding it high, I declare, "I'm going to frame this and put it up on my wall as a reminder of my addiction."

I stay with Kara for a week, until I feel calm and settled. *I can do this,* I tell myself. *I have quit drinking cold turkey countless times when I needed and wanted to. I am stronger than these pills. I don't want to do them anymore, and for all my life I've done only exactly what I wanted.*

Despite this grand gesture, I do not toss the pills.

I'm clearheaded and sober when I fly east to join Hillary's campaign the first week of January. Lena Dunham, the writer and actor, will be there, too, and before the event she sends me a text: "Do you have your speech all planned out?" I panic; I have no speech, not even a loose outline prepared, and so I text my agent: "What speech? You didn't tell me I need to have a speech, like a proper speech." His response is immediate and reassuring: "No, it's not a proper speech. It's what you do—you just do your thing. You just go. You're the best at it."

When we arrive in Portsmouth, New Hampshire, I speak first. I say that being able to envision a female in the Oval Office is exactly what I've been working toward my whole life. I've just retired from playing professional soccer, something that wasn't even possible fifteen years ago, and now here we are, possibly having a woman as president. Scratch that—it's not *if* Hillary gets into office, but *when*.

I wait for raucous cheers and applause to subside.

I don't support Hillary just because she's a woman, I continue. I wholeheartedly believe that our country, by and large, is socially conscious, and if you examine her plans and ideas and goals, it makes sense to vote for her. And I believe that everyone is inherently worthy of opportunity; everyone deserves a chance. Even if you are a minority, even if you are a woman, even if you are different colors, different races, different orientations. And to me, she represents someone who gives all minorities in our country a positive mind-set: if she can do it, I can, too.

More cheers and applause, and then I bring it home:

The symbolism of a female president is incredibly exciting to me. Imagine a fifteen-year-old girl looking up to a woman president and walking a little taller, feeling a bit more confident, beginning to image that *she,* too, could achieve that office. And then imagine a fifteen-year-old boy, looking at his classmate and thinking she could be president one day—a slight shift in gender norms that could have a long-term ripple effect, eventually changing the world and the way we all operate in it. It's very exciting, and I'm looking forward to watching Hillary Clinton make it happen.

Lena approaches me afterward and says, "I think you're the most charismatic person I've listened to speak, ever."

"Come on," I protest, rolling my eyes.

"No," she insists. "You're really good at what you do."

I think of all the people she must know—writers and actors and artists who get paid to craft and deliver words. I am honored by the compliment, and impressed that she went out of her way to tell me.

"Thank you," I say, simply, and remind myself that I am proving myself in a venue that has nothing to do with soccer, that my value did not end when I stepped off the field. *I can do this,* I think. *I* am *doing this.*

While I build my new platform, researching equality issues and meeting people, my marriage continues to flounder. Sarah is angry at me for leaving Portland so abruptly, for temporarily blocking her number, for choosing to run away rather than face our problems head-on. When we do text, our words are stilted, and hint at the best way to dissolve our union rather than repair it. I have no idea what I need or even what I want, and I share my misery and confusion with Kara.

"It's so sad," I text. "It's hard to quit her and the life that we built. But it became a fantasy and not reality. That is what I do know now. It's been so hard to keep silent from her. Like the hardest thing I've ever done, in addition to not abusing pills and alcohol during that time. It makes me mad, tho. Loving someone so much that you actually have to let them go."

"Yep, the worst," Kara agrees.

"And I won't ever stop loving her."

"Honest answer," Kara writes. "You still off the pills?"

"Yes," I respond, truthfully. "But today I wanted anxiety ones after Sarah's e-mail. Hahahaha. Had a drink on the plane. That was it, tho. I want to get fit again. So I am gonna focus on that. ☺."

But my mind inevitably returns to the negative, exhuming the thoughts I've worked so hard to bury. Within a half hour I'm texting Kara again: "I have known for my whole life I wanted to be a mother. And I'm so mad that I can't do that right now. I've waited for years to be done playing for that experience. And I can't blame Sarah. It's my fault, too."

Kara encourages me to go away, carve out some time to reflect and relax, and to keep relying on my friends rather than on pills. "If you really want to find yourself," she writes, "you need to enroll everyone that you keep close to you."

"A retreat could be the answer," I concede. "I have to stop worrying about the plan I used to have about what my retirement was gonna look like."

"Surround yourself with people that you can grow with,"

she urges. "People who challenge you and don't give you a hall pass on being your best self."

"I have to accept what I hear . . . we are our environment. And Sarah challenged me to be a better person and not continue doing my patterns. I didn't want to change for her. That's why I left. I want to change for me. I know I married her because she would never let me get too lost. But here I am, needing to do it alone . . . I am lost. And it's okay. I accept that this is my life."

"AND you can be in action about getting found," Kara insists.

"I want to be stronger," I write. "I need help."

"Dude, it's not a failure to ask for help. Why not go quietly into a retreat center that focuses on restoring identity? Look into the Chopra Center. It's massage and yoga and organic food and silence. Let me help you get the help."

I think about the Rochester retirement party, that idolized version of myself that everyone believes is the real me. There's so much I want to do, and yet so much I want to undo, and I don't know how to reconcile the two.

"I have to hold my younger self and love on her," I answer.

Kara knows exactly what I mean. "Hold her in your arms and tell her. Ask for her forgiveness. She's your pure self. The un-jaded one."

"I know," I write, and can't help but smile thinking about her; in my mind, my childhood self is an entirely different person. "She was so cute and always needing a shower. Haha. The one who has never had her heart broken. I have to learn how to be alone. And be okay with it."

"You know how you always say you're unlovable?" she asks.

"I know logically I'm lovable," I reply, and think of how that worry plagued me as a kid—knowing I was different, and believing that difference was a liability. "But deep down I have a scar from long ago."

"Forgiveness is an act of self-love," she says. "You've suffered enough. You owe it to yourself, dude."

I have to muster the will to type my next words: "My self-loathing has been killing me."

"You're coming down now," she points out. "You're slowing down and processing it . . . I understand self-loathing. However, don't stay too long with that. There's no power there. There never will be."

"I want peace," I say, exhausted from the exchange. "Deep peace nothing can shake."

Toward the end of January, I take Kara's advice and rent a house in Manhattan Beach for three weeks, intending to decompress and center myself, to start off the New Year in a positive frame of mind. This year, 2016, is the year of the monkey, and I was born in 1980, another year of the monkey, which I take as a good omen. I plan to spend part of the time by myself, and I invite a group of friends, including Sydney, to join me for the rest. I am excited for my friends to see me in a state where I'm not crazy and weird and all doped up. I hire our World Cup chef to come cook healthy meals. Those three weeks will cost more than a year's worth of mortgage on my house in Portland, but it's worth every cent.

When Suzi the chef arrives, she goes shopping for organic fruits and vegetables and gathers us all in the kitchen while she does her magic. I take pictures of her beautiful meals and post them on Instagram, ignoring the commenters who ask why Sarah isn't there with me. I surf and post pictures of myself in my wet suit, and ignore more questions about Sarah. I think about who I was with her versus who I am by myself: *Am I afraid of being alone because I love Sarah, or because I'm just afraid of being alone? Was she my rock, or was I my rock, and I gave her more power than she should have had?* Every night I sit on the balcony and watch the sunset, taking comfort in knowing that the same view will greet me again tomorrow.

In the middle of my stay, I travel to Mexico for a weekend to attend a friend's wedding. I'm still abstaining from pills, but I stand at the bar and do shot after shot after shot. Kara's there, and she watches as I fall on the dance floor, slamming so hard on the ground that I break my finger; it crooks, witchlike, in the wrong direction. Without any hesitation, and feeling no pain, I stand up and break it back the other way, setting it in its proper place, and I celebrate this feat with another shot.

In February I decide to attempt complete sobriety, forgoing alcohol along with the pills. I visit my parents at their condo in Florida, intending to help my mother rehabilitate from knee surgery and further contemplate the state of my marriage. Sarah and I are at least texting again, taking inventory of what went wrong, like claims adjusters surveying rubble from a hurricane. Okay, we acknowledge, we really had something good, and we fucked it up. Either we accept what happened and move forward together, or we accept what happened and move apart. At the moment we're apart more than not, taking turns staying in the Portland house, leaving before the other one arrives.

I meditate with my mala beads and ask myself hard questions: *Can I accept responsibility for the things that happened, the things I caused? Can I accept responsibility for the hurt I've caused? That's why people get divorced—because they can't deal with the sad feelings they created. And until you can get right and accept the fact that you've shattered somebody, that you've broken their heart in more ways than one, there's no way that you're ever going to be able to survive.*

I start a new diet, the alkaline diet, with the goal of achieving an even pH balance by eliminating acidic foods: coffee, cheese, meats, refined sugars and flours, white bread. Certainly no muffins, booze, or prescription pills. *It's only thirty days,* I tell myself. *I'm an extremist; I can do anything for thirty days*. I am addicted to this diet while I'm on it, 100 percent committed, and I figure—while I'm at it—that I should work on balancing my obsessive personality.

I continue meditating, unleashing my thoughts: *I need to*

work on the balance of letting go a bit and letting other people be themselves. I did not let Sarah be herself.

I keep waiting for the thoughts to tire themselves out, to sit down and take a rest. But still they come, rattling through my mind with the urgency and reliability of an express train.

Pills will stop them, I think, but manage another day without them.

I spend two hours signing soccer balls, posters, and T-shirts. I go golfing with my dad. I take my mom to her physical therapy appointments and recall a conversation we had shortly after my last game; she could read the misery in every line on my face, every movement of my body. "Abby," she'd said, "I am your mom and it's okay not to be okay."

"Mom," I protested, "it's *not* okay for me not to be okay. And I don't feel comfortable talking about not being okay with many people." And then I said something as difficult for me to admit as it was for her to hear: "I especially don't feel comfortable talking about it with you, because I do still feel a sense of abandonment from my childhood, a fear that I was and am unlovable and unloved."

Now, two months later, I realize that voicing those thoughts was a breakthrough in our relationship, one I'd been wanting and working toward for years. *I do feel comfortable talking about it with her,* I think, *because I actually had that conversation. I let her see me at my worst and let her hear me admit it. And I came to Florida to help her heal, but she is also helping me.*

I check my phone for texts from Sarah, who's off snowboarding for the week with friends, and I fear she and I will never go away together again. I fear we'll never even live together again.

I last without the pills until March.

On the weekend of March 11, I fly out to Kansas City to see Sydney and her husband. She's pregnant with their first baby and has planned a gender reveal party, and I want to be there, for both her and myself. I want the contact high of someone else's joy, and the possibility of taking some of that feeling home.

I stay for four days so Sydney and I can have some time alone. I've long had a private rationale for binges and benders—*I'll quit when I get pregnant, because the baby will force me sober*—and the reminder that I'm not already there pervades every thought. We're talking for hours, just like the old days, but she's looking at me strangely, as if I'm speaking some language only I can understand. I brush it off and launch into a funny story, but her strange look persists.

"You've already told me," she says.

I brush it off and launch into another funny story.

"You've already told me," she says.

I brush it off and launch into another funny story. From her expression I can tell what she's thinking; she's heard this one, too. This time she takes pity on me and lets me prattle on.

After the rest of the guests have left, and we've picked up every last scrap of blue confetti, Sydney says we need to have a talk. She tells me she'd intended to ask me to be her son's godmother, but she can't until I get help and get sober. I've needed help for a long time, and she's only now finding the strength to tell me. She loves me, she's not judging me, and she'd do anything to help me bring myself back.

I have to catch my flight but can't bear to stop the conversation; I am desperate to hear the hard things.

"I'm having a breakdown," I text her, "because I know what I need to do. Give me strength. Please, I'm begging you. In a taxi to my house. And it will be empty without Sarah the whole time, but I'm just so confronted by it all right now."

"Take deep breaths," she responds, "and just believe that everything will be okay because it will be and it always is. You always told me that 'In the end it'll be okay.' You said that to me a million times and now you have to believe it."

"Okay, I will breathe," I write, inhaling as I type. "I want my life back. I have to love myself again, which I have started to really do. No joke. Just being here makes me feel like a child, and brings up all these emotions that make me feel crazy as fuck. I want you to know I need to lean on you and for you to tell me the hard things I need to hear. Don't tell me what will make me feel better in the moment, but what will make me a better person. I know you have always done that. Need it more now than ever."

I'm relieved to see the message bubble; she's still there.

"I want you to be happy again," she says. "And you're not

happy, you're just numb. I can't imagine how hard this is but you are NOT alone. If you need me to fly to Portland right now or to follow you around because you're scared of what it feels like to be alone in your own thoughts, I am right there with you. Pregnant or not, I am there."

"Thanks, Syd," I type. "In tears reading this. But I am strong and haven't been for so so long. I will get stronger. That I know. I have been getting stronger. It's just that being here makes it hard again, you know? I love you and thank you for loving me for just being me and my crazy self."

The taxi pulls up to my beautiful, custom home, quiet and empty. I sit at my kitchen table and can't bring myself to move. I pull out my phone and text Syd again: "I have been choosing to be sad. I know it. Hoping a miracle would happen . . . I know what needs to happen to truly move on. And running wasn't the answer."

Thankfully she's still there: "It never is," she says.

"But it lessened the toxicity."

"Seriously, the only thing that's going to help is time."

"I'm impatient. And I hate that I have this fucking fancy home. I built this for my future, and now it's empty with no love." I think about the other future I've been building—the advocacy platform, the old girls' club—and share a fear I hadn't been able to admit, even to myself: "I'm afraid my life won't lend me to any truly loving relationships. I can make myself as busy as I want, and I will because it's all I know . . . My schedule, Syd. And what I do and will do. No one would want that."

"You WILL!" she insists. "Because you deserve it. Someone who loves you for exactly who you are and not who they want you to be."

I feel an urge to confess sins she already knows: "I drank too much, Syd. Because I felt her disconnect and me disconnect. I did that, too. I took pills because I couldn't deal."

"Yeah," she agrees, "and that's something that you're still living with that can be fixed."

"How do I sell this house then? And how do I move on? I want happy again."

She offers practical advice: "You sell the house. You move to wherever you want, and you pick yourself up off the ground as you've done many times before, and you put one foot in front of the other. That is the only way. And you put your heart and soul into being a better person for YOURSELF and no one else."

"Yeah, that sounds nice," I agree. "I want to love me again. Be proud of myself again."

I am brimming with resolve. I quit the pills again.

Two weeks later, Sydney receives a cryptic text from a friend: "OMG . . . Abby!"

Her first thought is that I had overdosed and died.

22

FAILURE

On the last day of March, Sarah and I have yet another blowout fight—one that convinces me, finally, that we are really and truly over. We stand in our kitchen, in the lovely, loveless house, and hurl our words, each one sharper and more brutal than the last. We've created a mess that extends beyond the two of us, with all our friends having to choose sides and split their time. I am being ostracized from my city, exiled from my own life, and I am both despondent and furious. It's been twelve days since I've taken a drink or a pill, and my pain, unhindered, now attacks me with a swift and thorough viciousness.

"This happened," I say. "This is happening. The least you can do is go and apologize to all our friends for putting them in such an uncomfortable, precarious position." With each breath I regain an inch of control. "Now I'm going to own my own fucking bullshit," I declare. "I'm drawing up divorce papers. I'll move out, you'll move out, I'll sell my car, you'll sell the other car, we'll get new shit, get new everything, and start over."

I seclude myself on the opposite side of our house, as far away from her as I can be without leaving. I am still distraught at the idea of selling but can't imagine staying here, trapped in four thousand square feet of ruined paradise, surrounded by the ghosts of dead dreams.

I am still sober, and furious, when I fall asleep.

The following morning I awaken with a sense of purpose and resolution. There are practical tasks I must accomplish to move forward. I pack up my most valuable possessions, stashing them all in my car. I search online for an interim apartment to rent, anyplace that's clean and will accept me quickly, and get a hotel room downtown. I wander the hallways, feeling like I'm on the road in my own city, the sole member of my own visiting team. I narrowly avoid the minibar and don't unpack my stash of pills.

Exhausted, I send a group text to some friends, confirming plans to meet for a game of golf the next day.

When I awaken, I know exactly where I am and what I left behind. I remain invigorated by the act of seizing control, by creating distance between my past and future. I shop for roomfuls of furniture online and venture out to buy a new bed, arranging for expedited shipping to the rented apartment. As a small, petty act of revenge, I compose a cheerful tweet about my spree: "Just got the best and quickest help from Lindsey at Bedmart. Go check them out!!!!" accompanied by a photo of my new mattress.

When I arrive at the golf club, I decide I've earned a few drinks, two on the front nine and two on the back. Although I haven't eaten much, I am feeling pleasant and soft around the edges but not at all drunk. A friend invites the entire group for dinner, and I hitch a ride to his house, leaving my car behind. We cook and laugh and drink wine; I have three glasses in three hours and very little food. When I get up to leave around 11 P.M., my friends urge me to call an Uber, just to be safe.

"I promise I will," I say, and it's one of the few times in my life I tell a successful lie. I have about two hundred thousand dollars' worth of valuables and important paperwork in my car—watches, rings, bank statements, cash, trophies, Olympic medals—and I don't want to risk a smash and grab. I do the math: I've been out since 1 P.M., which means seven drinks in ten hours. The walk back to the golf club is a quarter of a mile, and the crisp night air makes me feel fresh and alert.

I just want to get back to my hotel room and lie in a bed that Sarah's never touched.

I drive down a hill toward an unfamiliar part of Portland, glancing intermittently at my GPS. I hear the chirp of a siren before I see the flashing lights; I'm being pulled over but am not sure why. The review mirror catches the beams, sweeping them across my face, and I tilt my chin upward to meet my own gaze. Panic is etched in every feature—eyes widened, mouth slack, skin drained of blood—to a degree that I am nearly unrecognizable. *I'm fine,* I remind myself. *This will be all cleared up soon and I'll be on my way.*

We perform the standard routine: I ask what seems to be the problem, officer, and he requests my license and registration, explaining that I ran through a red light. Later, I'll recreate my steps, driving through this intersection, and notice that the branches of low-lying trees dip into my sightline, obscuring my view.

As he scans the documents, he asks if I've been drinking. I tell him I've just come from a dinner party, where I had a few glasses of wine.

"Okay," he says. "Well, your eyes are bloodshot, and I smell booze on your breath."

He asks me to submit to a field sobriety test, and I agree.

As I step out of the car, he calls another cop and reports our location. This second officer, the field test cop, has one job—traveling from drunk call to drunk call—and it takes ten minutes for him to arrive. While we wait I am proper and polite, full of *yes, sirs* and apologies, my mother's ceaseless drills about manners rising like cream to the surface.

The field test cop gets down to business, walking me behind the car. Holding a flashlight aloft, he intones instructions: "Follow the tip of my pen with only your eyes."

He waves his pen and I follow the light, instinctively moving my head.

"Only your eyes," he reminds me.

"I'm sorry," I say, and force my head to remain absolutely still, my eyes flicking left and right, up and down.

I am sure I passed, but it's not over; next he ushers me to the sidewalk to walk the line.

"Okay," he says. "I'm going to watch you walk heel to toe for nine steps forward, and then nine steps back, counting out loud both times."

A busy highway stretches below us, just to the right, and the noise makes it difficult to decipher his words. I'm terrified of misunderstanding, like I did when I followed the light, so I ask him to demonstrate the walk. He walks four steps and totters a bit, and stops before he can show me the proper way to turn.

"Are you serious?" I ask. "You can't even do it."

"Just do it," he says, and I understand I have no choice.

I start, mimicking his steps, and realize the sidewalk is sloped, badly enough that I would have trouble passing this test even in broad daylight with no alcohol in my system. After four steps I also veer off the line. I look up at the officer and shrug, as if to say *What did you expect?,* but his expression makes it clear: my stumble is the only one that matters.

Without warning, I feel my arms yanked back and metal against my wrists, my hands meeting at the small of my back.

"Whoa!" I say, turning sideways. "Hey, what's going on?"

"You're under arrest for driving under the influence of intoxicants," he says.

My mouth is dry with panic, my breath coming in gasps. *This is clearly a misunderstanding,* I tell myself. *I can explain. I can talk my way through this.* When I speak, I sound more frantic than I want to: "Holy shit! Wait a second. We need to talk about this. I swear to God I am not fucking drunk. I'm not saying that just to get off. I *promise* you I am not drunk."

He remains unconvinced. "Well, we need to take you down to the station for a Breathalyzer examination."

"I need to speak to a lawyer," I say. "This is crazy."

Another officer, a woman, appears from behind. My arms are jerked again and there's a *click* as the handcuffs cinch tighter, the metal grinding against my wrist bones.

I twist, trying to meet her gaze. "Not for nothing," I say, "but could you please loosen these handcuffs? They're very tight. They're entirely too tight for someone who is not resisting arrest."

She doesn't look at me. "Get in the car," she orders, making each word its own sentence. Reaching up, she palms my head and pushes me down into the squad car. The cuffs dig into my back. I lean forward, my head nearly touching the divider. I'm a caged pet, groveling for attention, hoping they can understand my attempts at communication. "Can you please move my car to a proper parking spot," I ask, "and bring my black backpack to me?" They grant me those small mercies and my backpack comes along for the ride, carrying two Olympic gold medals and my wedding ring, shiny vestiges of my former life.

This is not happening right now, I think. *This is a fucking nightmare.* Out loud I say, "I've never been in a police car before. This is the worst thing that's ever happened to me."

They don't respond, and for the rest of the trip I am quiet.

The police station is a tight white box, each wall tilting in and encroaching on my space. I am escorted to a window where I recite my name and other pertinent information, and then to a cell. The door swings shut. Another small mercy: a guard slips my cell phone through the bars so I can make phone calls. My first is to a friend who is a lawyer, who refers me to a lawyer friend of his who specializes in DUI law. That number rings and rings. No answer. Next I call Sarah. *Please pick up, please pick up,* I plead silently. *I know you hate me right now but please pick up.*

She does. "I'll be right there," she says, and I almost can't believe it. *I don't deserve this,* I think. *I don't deserve her.* Whatever she did, I was complicit. I wasn't there; I chose instead to be with alcohol and pills.

The booking officer strolls past the cell. "Excuse me," I call out. "My lawyer isn't answering."

"All right," he says, and returns with the yellow pages. It is the sight of that fat book, the pages flipped to the "A" section for attorneys, that finally cracks me. *What the fuck?* I think. *What is happening right now? My life is literally falling through my fingertips.* In the moment I can't even accuse myself of being hyperbolic, having spent all of my thirty-five years being the special one, the different one, the one—*yes*—with the world at her fingertips, and now, with the heft of that yellow book in my palm, I picture it all rewinding, event by event, stopping at the beginning, with my five-year-old self on the soccer field, legs now pinwheeling backward instead of forward, my feet never touching the ball.

I start crying, long, jagged sobs that scorch the back of my throat, and I don't care who sees or hears me. I am crying so hard that some guard takes pity and brings me a glass of water, explaining that forcing yourself to drink makes your body stop crying. For once I drink it greedily, and by the time I take my last gulp it's worked its magic, calming me down enough to pick up my ringing phone. It's my lawyer, who advises me to take the Breathalyzer test; if I refuse, they'll issue a warrant forcing me to give a blood sample instead. My blood sample, he explains, will reveal with inarguable specificity exactly what's running through my veins right now, while the Breathalyzer is an imperfect test. And if I refuse the Breathalyzer, I'll lose my license immediately for a year, according to Portland law. Before we hang up, he reminds me that I have the right to refuse to answer any questions they might ask.

The Breathalyzer it is, I think. I am confident it will show I am below the legal limit.

I follow an officer into the test area, passing a clock along the way: just after midnight. I open my mouth and he shines a light inside, making me lift my tongue to prove there's nothing underneath. With the device hovering by my mouth, I close my eyes and blow. The number says .142; the legal limit is .08.

That can't be right, I think. *No fucking way.*

Two and a half minutes pass, and I'm instructed to blow again; this time it reads .131. "Wait," I say. "There's a huge discrepancy—for two and a half minutes—between .142 and .131. Based on my calculation, in ten minutes I'll be under the legal limit. That doesn't make any sense."

"It's pretty common," the officer says.

"All right, but I don't believe this is pretty common. This is my first time ever doing this, and I don't trust this thing. My life is in the hands of this machine. And the machine is telling me that in ten minutes, I'll be under the legal limit. That is crazy to me."

The officer nods and smiles as though he's heard this tirade a thousand times. I'm led out of the room and through a series of doors. Along the way they take all my personal effects—watch, wallet, cell phone, my grandmother's ring—and seal them up. I start crying again, even harder than before, and someone appears with another glass of water, which pauses the tears long enough for a mug shot. My last public photos featured me playing a charity golf game with Caitlyn Jenner and jumping into a pond, showboating as if I'd scored a game-winning goal. I imagine the mug shot going out to the world, attached to thousands of tweets, featured on the news for all my nieces and nephews to see. *This is happening,* I think. *This is truth. Everything I've worked for is going to be lost.* As soon as the flash recedes, imprinting specks of light inside my closed eyes, I begin to cry again.

I'm led away, this time to a waiting room crammed with rows of chairs. Officers occupy a line of desks along the back. A partition separates the women's side from the men's, and each side has a blaring television set. The first person I see is a woman who's obviously a drug addict. She's tweaking, fingers grating her skin, narrating a story only she can follow. The room is freezing, sixty-something degrees, and I tuck my legs up to my chest, wrapping my arms around my shins. I lower my head to the points of my knees and rock myself back and forth. I think about Sarah, waiting outside for me in her car, ten thousand dollars in cash in her purse.

Within minutes I hear a cacophony of footsteps shuffling toward me, and I look up to see a half dozen pairs of shoes, all of them, strangely, without laces. *Weird,* I think, and my eye focuses on one pair in particular: a man's high-tops, the tongues so long they flap down to lick the tips of his toes. And then it hits me: no one is allowed to have shoelaces in jail because shoelaces are a potential deadly weapon, a means of suicide or murder. I wonder why they didn't take mine, too—they must realize, on some level, that I don't belong here. Then I look down at my feet and have my answer.

I'm wearing Birkenstocks.

Hours pass, feeling like days. The tongues of the man's sneakers still lap at his toes. The tweaker scratches at her skin as though it's a lottery card. I wait, and wait, and think of Sarah, still sitting out in the car. I am almost relieved when someone calls my name. I go to the window, where I'm told my information needs to be entered into the system. One by one my fingers are pressed against a screen, scanning and recording my fingerprints. A woman stands nearby, watching. I notice her name tag, which bears the initials JT. She's wearing civilian clothes and no gun; I assume she's a clerk.

"I need a number to call," she says. "I need to call someone to make sure all your information checks out."

I tell her I don't know my wife's number—it's programmed into my cell, which is in storage—and instead I give her my mother's land line, my old land line.

JT must see the panic in my face at the thought of calling home. She speaks softly, kindly, telling me it's going to be okay. They just have to run my fingerprints through the FBI database to make sure I have no outstanding warrants or DUIs. Standard procedure before I can be released on my own recognizance.

I return to my seat. I watch the clock, the minute hand moving with agonizing lethargy. I approach one of the desk officers. "I really, really would appreciate it if someone would go outside and check on my wife," I say. "She's out there sitting with a bunch of cash in a really bad part of town. If

I'm not going to get out of here until seven in the morning, I would really like for someone to just tell her to go home."

He agrees and picks up my backpack; he'll bring it out to her and tell her what I said. He's kind enough to return with her phone number, and points to a stainless steel phone in the waiting area. I can use it to call her collect.

"Please go home," I beg when she picks up. "It makes me feel better knowing you're safe."

She tells me she's not going anywhere.

The room is still freezing. I try to send my mind to another place: I'm at camp, preparing for a tournament. I speed-walk around the rows of chairs, doing laps, five in one direction before I spin around. I lean against the wall and sink down so my thighs are parallel to the floor, holding for two minutes. I watch my quad muscles flex. I realize I've yet to take a piss—how drunk could I possibly be? I do squats, more laps, more wall sits. I'm about to embark on another round when JT, the clerk, summons me over. She tells me I'm ready for release—she just has a few final questions.

"Are you on drugs?" she asks.

"No, I'm not on drugs," I say.

"Have you ever taken drugs?"

"What does this have to do with anything?" I ask, and think: *My lawyer has invoked my right to silence.*

"You need to answer these questions. Have you ever taken drugs?"

"Over ten years ago, but what does this have to do with tonight? I don't understand."

She looks up, pen poised over paper. "I have to ask these questions to make sure you're not going to hurt yourself or hurt anyone else."

I tell assure her that's not a possibility, but she presses on. Have I done heroin? No. Have I done meth? No. Have you ever done marijuana?

"Over ten years ago," I repeat. "I don't know what this has to do with anything."

Cocaine?

"Again," I say, "I don't know what this has to do with anything."

She's finished with me, finally, and I'm crying again. By the time I venture outside it's nearly dawn, a pink fingernail of sun inching up the sky, and Sarah is still there, waiting for me. The way she leans against the door of her Jeep—arms crossed, face expectant—reminds me of Jake at the end of *Sixteen Candles,* hoping it's not too late to get the girl, and suddenly I'm laughing instead.

23

HUMAN

I usually dread the morning after drinking. Who did I text? What did I post? What damage have I caused, what havoc have I wreaked? What don't I remember? What have I put out into the universe that will boomerang back to me? But on this morning after, I am fully aware of what I've done and what I need to do. First, I gather every pill bottle left in my stash, give them all to Sarah, and vow never to take one again.

As of this writing, I've kept that promise.

I make a list of all the people I've hurt and disappointed and reach out to them one by one. My mother tells me that things happen sometimes, and that I'm going to be okay, and that she loves me no matter what—always has and always will. I call my family in Rochester and tell them I'll come home that weekend; I want to gather all my nieces and nephews and talk to them candidly. Let this be a lesson, I'll tell them. Let me be an example. Let me explain all the ways you shouldn't be like me when you grow up.

I pick my public words just as carefully; I want them to sound like me—honest and straight, like someone willing to accept blame. I recognize a strange truth: after all the searching, the meditation, the drinking, the pills, the therapy, the solitary road trips, the tortured text exchanges, and the time spent living in my head, this colossal mistake will be the catalyst for getting to know myself again.

I post this paragraph on all my social media accounts:

> Last night I was arrested for DUI in Portland after dinner at a friend's house. Those that know me, know that I have always demanded excellence from myself. I have let myself and others down.
>
> I take full responsibility for my actions. This is all on me. I promise that I will do whatever it takes to ensure that my horrible mistake is never repeated.
>
> I am so sorry to my family, friends, fans and those that look to follow a better example.
>
> —Abby

Now that it's out there, I brace myself, waiting to see what will come back to me. I text with Kara, knowing she will help me sort through the mess I've made and challenge me to be my responsible self.

"Today is brutal," I text her on Monday afternoon. "Now I have to feel and accept this. I have hurt a lot of people with all this. Myself mostly, but I'm aware that I'm responsible for others' hurt, too."

"Yep, I get that," she responds, adding an emoji of mala beads. "Shaman's death, dude. There is a part of you that is being called to die so you can be and have everything you've ever wanted. Try to see this as a blessing."

"I'm so mad at myself that I got this far gone," I reply.

"I gotta tell you . . . people in your life have reached out to me throughout the past year. I never told you. There has been stuff going on behind the scenes that I feel like I can be open with you about now."

"I'm not surprised," I say. "Train wreck . . . and Sarah and I? I'm so all over the place."

"You gotta get clean," she urges. "It's number one. Don't worry about that right now . . . Abby, you're stubborn as fuck. You're super lucky and the Universe has given you a love tap."

"I know. And it's not a tap. Punch to the motherfucking face. Which I deserve."

"This is what you needed."

"I know," I admit. "I will need to be sober for one year. Which I pray will let me see life can be lived well and happy sober. I don't know where to even begin again with my life."

"Lean," she says, and includes a peace-fingers emoji. "And try not to lean on folks that will only agree with you."

"I know," I tell her. "That's why I have you, buddy. And I'm learning to find my own true north."

News trucks intermittently cruise by my house; I hide out in a coffee shop until they give up. A few of the players on the men's national team make pointed jokes. One of them tweets, "Must've been a foreign American player's fault," a reference to a comment I'd made about too many "foreign guys" playing for the U.S. team. His tweet launches its own debate. Although I stay offline, I'm thinking, *He's right. I'm an idiot and an asshole for driving under the influence.* A half hour later, that same player follows up with begrudging kindness: "I almost forgot that I have to be politically correct because I'm an athlete. We're human. Abby took full responsibility. Good."

Sydney calls and cries and tells me how relieved she is to hear my voice. Apologize to your body, she tells me. That remarkable, incredibly gifted vessel that has served you so well for so many years. Treat it well and let it heal; that's where your renewal begins.

As soon as we hang up I get a text from my brother-in-law, a firefighter, which I've read every day since my arrest and will continue to read for a long time to come:

> Abby, I'm sorry to hear and read about your situation. I can only imagine what you're going through. That being said, I offer the following: In the fire department, we see the damage and destruction that fires cause. Everyone always looks to the fire as the culprit, but the real enemy is the source. Some of the time, the source is obvious—the gas can left out, the cigarette in the ashtray, etc.—but the majority of the

time we have to dig. The source is hidden within the walls, in the foundation of the home. It smolders, unnoticed to everyone, until it reaches the point of ignition and explodes.

Your metaphoric house caught fire this weekend. I believe that the source has been building unnoticed, except by you, for a while now. The good news is that if you attack the source, you can prevent further fires. Treat this as you would any other injury you've had. Let the bones and tissues heal, just like it's an internal injury. Just as you've sought help before for your leg, you need to ask for help from your friends and family. You cannot do this on your own. Just like other injuries you've recovered from, this will be painful, frustrating, demoralizing. But you will get better. As with every fire I've gone to, you will rebuild and be in a better, safer place going forward.

I will get better, I think. *And I have no choice but to go forward.*

Embarrassing details trickle out: my mug shot, my experimentation with drugs, the legal repercussions after I plead guilty to driving under the influence of intoxicants. I choose to enter a diversion program, which involves drug and alcohol assessment and treatment. I lose my license for three months and have a Breathalyzer installed in my car. When I'm allowed to drive again, I'll have to blow in it to prove my sobriety before I can start the engine. The judge orders me to abstain from drinking any alcohol at all. The order isn't even necessary; I have no desire to drink. I'm in training again, this time preparing for the opponent within, the most formidable one I've ever faced. This time, instead of gaining speed I'm slowing down, unraveling all the excuses and lies, thawing everything I deadened and numbed. I've made so many decisions that have taken me away from myself, that have made it impossible to know who I am, and I'm ready to chart the path back. Intense Abby assures me I can succeed, and Chill Abby reminds me that a happy life still includes moments of pain.

As part of my program, I attend a victim impact panel, two hours of listening to people who made my same mistakes and others who've suffered as a result. It takes place one rainy Thursday night in an auditorium adjacent to the hospital. As soon as I sit down, the man next to me taps my shoulder.

"Are you Abby Wambach?" he asks.

I admit that I am.

He smiles and extends his hand. "When I saw you got arrested," he says, "it made me feel better about myself."

"Happy to help," I tell him, and we become fast friends.

First up is Antonio, who was stoned when he got into an accident, crushing one of his legs; he uses a self-described pimp cane to get around. Joan, in her fifties, was the victim of a drunk driver twenty years ago. She broke the windshield with her head, injuring her brain so traumatically she became a different person. Likes became dislikes; long-held opinions changed; certainties morphed into questions. She had to relearn how to eat, walk, tie her shoes, comb her hair, brush her teeth.

I cry throughout her talk, realizing what I could have done to someone. I realize how thankful I am that I got caught in time.

John walks down the aisle led by a black lab. At first I think it's a service animal, but he reveals that the dog belonged to his son and daughter-in-law, who were both killed by a drunk driver. Instead of raising his son, he's now raising his grandson.

I cry again.

The last speaker is a judge—"Judge Amy"—who says she's not here to lecture us, to tell us to quit whatever vices led us here today. She just wants us to stop and think: everything we saw and heard about in this session was 100 percent preventable. We have the power and the control. We can choose never to sit in these seats again.

I offer to withdraw from my scheduled speaking engagements, but they all still want me to come. I attend the People Analytics Conference at Wharton, an event I'd planned at the height of my addiction, and I'm grateful to be onstage with a clear mind, a sharper picture of who I am and what I can contribute. I fear it's not much—I feel out of my league among these brilliant academics—but afterward Adam Grant says he admires the way I handled the DUI. If I'm interested, he'd like me to return to teach a class on creative management, emphasizing authenticity and the power in confronting your past. I tell him I'd be thrilled; by then, I might be an expert myself.

I especially appreciate speaking at colleges, where the audiences are people who have yet to make their worst decision, people who can still learn from my own. At each school—the University of Kentucky, Penn State, and Georgetown—the auditoriums are filled with students willing to hear what I have to say. Each time, my mind rewinds to one of my first postretirement appearances: the kids' community soccer league, where the negative commentary scrolled through my brain and I felt like a fraud. As always, I have no speech prepared, and when the light drops down on my head, following me across the stage, I do what I've always done and just start talking, hoping the words land right.

I talk about my family and being raised on competition, the bruises that covered my body after long days playing with my brothers. I talk about my first devastating failure, losing the state high school championship, and how it propelled me to try harder and never give up. I talk about how it paid off the following year, during my rookie season at Florida, when—precocious little shit that I was—I took over my team's huddle and announced that we're not fucking losing to these bitches. I talk about breaking my leg before the 2008 Olympics: the difficulty in staying home, the humility in realizing that my team didn't need me to win. I talk about my last World Cup and the hard, cold realization of knowing my time was almost up, that the one defining skill of my life had faded and dulled. I talk about summoning the will to lead from the bench, telling younger players to seize their chance that the future is theirs to define.

Then I flip the conversation, addressing the students directly. You should defy labels, I tell them, whether imposed by others or yourselves. You should become comfortable with conflict and disagreement. You should not be afraid to speak your mind. You're going to be the catalyst for real change. The world is out there, waiting to hear your voices and mark your steps. It's not your failures that define you, but how you react to them and use them to change. You should all ask yourselves three questions: Where do you want to go, how do you want to get there, and why?

This time, I believe my own words, and am on my way to finding the answers.

EPILOGUE

It's early, the sun still too low to cast shadows, and I'm running along the streets of Paris, letting myself get lost, a routine I established as soon as I arrived. Soccer has taken me all over the world but never allowed me to see it beyond the hotel rooms and training facilities and fields. So though I've visited Paris many times, this ancient city is new to me. It suits me, this atmosphere of discovery, of not knowing where every twisty path might lead. In the three months since my arrest I've felt new to myself, open to whatever I might find—good or bad, soothing or disconcerting, familiar or strange.

I'm here for three weeks, covering the Euros—Europe's championship tournament for men's soccer—for my new job with ESPN. Soon after I landed, my colleagues invited me to meet them in the bar of the Hotel Pont Royal. I was prepared for the inevitable question—Do I want a drink?—and I responded the same way I have since I quit: "I'm not drinking, I'll have water." I launched into my customary follow-up explanation, laced with self-deprecating jokes: "I'm not drinking because I got a DUI, as everyone knows, and clearly drinking wasn't working for me. I tried like hell to make it work for me. No person on the planet has tried harder to be good at drinking, and yet all of my practice amounted to nothing." Something new and strange: realizing I will never again be the main spectacle at the party, the engine that makes it go, and not missing that role at all.

A few moments later, one colleague approached and said he's been sober for twenty-something years, and I'm welcome to accompany him to a meeting anytime. Another followed, and made sure no one else was listening when he offered this advice: I don't have to keep bringing up my DUI. I shouldn't feel like I need to explain or justify my behavior. No one needs to be comfortable with my motivations but me.

I thanked him, and had another moment of recognition: I don't need to justify my behavior, to acknowledge the messiness of my past, but I *want* to. Talking about it wrests away the control it's had over me. Talking about it razes the shame, leaving room for another emotion to rise in its place.

The Eiffel Tower looms to my right. My data watch beeps alerts about my heart rate and speed, a sound that will always be familiar. I cross the bridge to the south side of the Seine and pick up speed, weaving around pedestrians, catching snatches of mysterious conversation. I pass floating gardens, the Musée d'Orsay, the Louvre. At the Pont des Arts, the bridge famously weighted with thousands of love locks, I think of Sarah, back in Portland, in the house I still don't call home.

All of our anger and resentment and blame, smoldering for years, have finally put themselves out. When the smoke cleared, and my sobriety allowed me to excavate my feelings, I admitted all of my faults—both what I'd done and what I failed to do. I never gave her enough credit for encouraging me to confront my issues. I never gave myself fully to her, because I'd long ago given myself to soccer. I tried to split my time and devotion between the two and ended up failing at both. Our future together is still uncertain, but now the good memories have asserted themselves, reminding us why we once worked so well, and of the gifts we've given each other. I've spent my whole life running—from pain, from fear, from myself—and without her I never would have stopped.

On my fourth day here, I arrived at the studio to provide my first commentary on a game, Slovakia versus Wales. I am used to performing for an audience but my body has always done the work; even as I sunk into my chair, I worried my mind might not be up to the task. The men's game is foreign territory, with its own history and nuances and rules, and it will take time to know it as well as I know my own game. So I approached the job as I approach everything: from the gut. *I'm going to stick to what I know and what I'm good at,* I told myself. *And what I'm good at is bullshitting.*

Moments after the camera began rolling, I realized my mistake. *Wow,* I thought. *That was epically horrible.* Another realization: I don't know if I'll ever be skilled at this, no matter how hard I try, and that's okay. I'm not always going to be good, I'm not always going to win, and I'm no longer afraid of failure.

I keep running. I pass the gargoyles of Notre Dame, pensive and menacing and hideous. I veer off into a labyrinth of alleys, long stretches of cobblestones that seem to narrow with each step, as if leading to the point of a cone. Storefronts blur past: fromageries, boulangeries, pâtisseries, the last a reminder that I'm still forgoing muffins. At the end of one path a woman looks at me, and does a double-take. She waves me down, and I stop, my breath loud in my ears.

"Are you Abby Wambach? The soccer player?"

I'm in France! I think. *Are you serious?* My ego can't help but preen as I acknowledge that yes, I am. Silently I correct her—*I'm not a soccer player anymore*—but then I realize she's right. Soccer is no longer what I do, but it will always be a part of who I am, an indispensable thread of my past. I can't deny it any more than I can deny the labels I've claimed in this book: fraud, rebel, wife, advocate, addict, failure, human—all of them. They'll always be there, stitched into my psyche, even as I make room for new labels, ones I've yet to discover and claim.

I wave to the woman and run off, anonymous once again. The maze unfurls itself before me, beckoning. I realize I know where I am, and how to find my way back.

ACKNOWLEDGMENTS

There are so many people in my life that inked the words to these pages. Your love and teachings and support are not lost on me. Thank you is wildly insufficient when it comes to my true, deep feelings for you all. I love you ALL.

My Family, My Body:
To Mom, Dad, Beth, Laura, Peter, Matt, Pat, Andy, Brooke, Tracy, all my in-laws and nieces and nephews . . . I have learned so many beautiful things along the way, and have felt your love and support through all my life adventures. Thank you for letting me go wander, yet always having a place to call HOME.

My chosen Family, My Spirit:
To Sarah, Are, Dena, Kara, Syd, Breaca, Audrey, Al . . . There are actually NO WORDS! You have carried my heart in yours, and the space you have allowed me to BE myself, and the learning and love I have felt in you, has shaped the person I am, but more important the person I want to become. My love for you is unending.

My work Family, My Mind:
I want to thank my editor Julia Cheiffetz and the team at HarperCollins including Lynn Grady, Sean Newcott, and Katie Steinberg. Writing this book was an intense process and I am indebted to Karen Abbott for her patience and brilliance in helping me tell my story. To Dan, all my teammates and coaches. . . I have spent most of my adult life with you all, and I have learned a great many things. I've learned what hard work actually looks like, and that it sometimes isn't always pretty. I learned that no matter how badly you want to achieve anything in life, that the way in which you go about achieving it is actually the most important thing. Having this fierce integrity will always be with me for all of my life.

To THE love of my life . . .

Here is to the next 1,000 years.

ABOUT THE AUTHOR

ABBY WAMBACH is an American soccer player, two-time Olympic gold medalist, Women's World Cup Champion, and the 2012 FIFA World Player of the Year. A six-time winner of the U.S. Soccer Athlete of the Year award, Wambach has been a regular on the U.S. Women's National Soccer Team since 2003, earning her first cap in 2001. She is the highest all-time scorer for the U.S. Women's National Team and holds the world record for international goals for both female and male soccer players, with 184. A true leader on and off the field, Wambach is dedicating the next chapter of her career to fighting for equality and inclusion.